To my Mother

Mātā mittaṁ sake ghare
S I 37

Encounters with Buddhism

Edited and with an Introduction by
Shravasti Dhammika

Graham Brash

C S Dhammika - first edition 1990
                 second edition 1991

First published in 1990 by Buddhist Research Society
This edition published in 1991 by
Graham Brash (Pte) Ltd
227 Rangoon Road
Singapore 0821

ISBN 9971-49-270-9

Cover design by Beatrice Ling
Typeset by Quaser Technology Pte Ltd
Printed in Singapore by Elka Printing Service

Contents

Acknowledgements

I would like to thank all those who have contributed
their stories to this book, for without their willingness to
talk about what is, after all something very personal, it
would not have seen the light of day. I would also like
to thank Lisa Reinhart, Wynne Kline and Philip Tan for
all the advice and time they have given in helping to
prepare the manuscript. Finally, I would like to thank
Venerable B. Dhammaratana for his constant encouragement.

Preface

Fourteen writers here describe how they came to be Buddhists. Men and women of different nationalities: each tells the story of his or her encounter with Buddhism and of how they became a Buddhist. Together they form an interesting and significant piece of documentation of what are undoubtedly some important ethical, religious and philosophical trends among Buddhists in the latter half of the twentieth century.

Those who are familiar with the variety of ways in which Buddhism has, virtually in this century, become a 'world religion' in a sense in which it was not previously, will recognise in these biographical accounts the kinds of examples which could no doubt be repeated many times over. One feature which seems to characterise most of the cases described here, and makes them representative of the wider company of today's *new* adherents to Buddhism, is that the majority of them are tertiary-educated, some in the humanities and some, perhaps slightly more, in the sciences. This is not to say that the increase in the number of Buddhists in various places is always or necessarily associated with young, upwardly-mobile, tertiary-educated persons, but that such people *do* form a significant part of that increase. Others in the twentieth century have been attracted to Buddhism for what the Buddhist community and a Buddhist identity offered them in the way of social emancipation: such, for example, were the Untouchable-class followers of Dr. Ambedkar in India in the 1950s.

Another substantial subdivision among these writers is that practically two thirds of them (64%) became Buddhists in their twenties. It also happens that they were in their twenties in the decade of the 1970s. It is possible that different periods have their special and religious characteristics, and that the decade of the seventies was one in which Westernised young people were responding to a mood which encouraged experimentation and novelty in personal attitudes and affiliations. While this in no way need suggest that *peer pressure* should be seen as an explanation, it is possible that attitudes in one decade, rather than say in a later decade, tend to offer what may be called a certain measure of '*peer encouragement*' to move in this or that direction, in terms of culture, behaviour or ideology. It is too early at present, and certainly from so small a sample of cases as we have here, to conclude that the 1970s and certainly the 1980s will not eventually be seen to have been similarly significant for Buddhist affiliation and growth.

If any hypothesis may be constructed on the admittedly rather slender basis of this sample, it is that, for whatever reason, the decade of the 1970s seem to have been specially favourable for 'becoming a Buddhist' and that in that decade, as in others, it was within the age range 20 to 30 that most of the decisions recorded here were made.

Before 'becoming Buddhist', *eleven out of the fourteen were Christian by religion.* Of these eleven Christians, three had been Protestants, three Catholics and five 'Christian' unspecified. Of the three who had previously *not* been Christian, one had been a Muslim, one an agnostic, and one 'no religion'.

One important and fairly obvious reason why so high a proportion of these cases of becoming a Buddhist are written by those who were formerly of Christian identity may be that a high proportion of the cases (64%) are of Anglo-American origin, and that their stories *are written in English*. However, from what is, in sociological terms, so small a sample, it would be unwise to attempt to draw other than tentative conclusions. Nevertheless, it would be interesting to see the results of further research on the question of to what extent the affirming of a *positive* Buddhist identity is increasing also among non-anglophones. But that, so to speak, is another story. What the reader will find sufficiently fascinating, no doubt, are the stories recorded here.

Prof Trevor Ling
Institute of South East
Asian Studies.

Introduction

The phenomenon of conversion as it is understood in the religious context means the acceptance of a new set of beliefs or practices. Buddhism recognizes two levels or intensities of conversion - mundane and transcendental - the first not necessarily leading to the second, but the second almost always preceded by the first. Mundane conversion is not dissimilar to conversion as it is understood in other religious traditions. It is an intellectual appreciation of the Buddha's teaching, leading to its practice and application. However, at this level, even though there might be dramatic changes in one's life, and even though one is heading in the right direction, utter freedom of mind, the ultimate goal of Buddhism, is still not a foregone conclusion.

But in time, with practice comes realization, and one begins to get glimpses of the truths taught by the Buddha, not just intellectually, but directly. The wall of ignorance begins to crumble and it is only a matter of time before it collapses completely, allowing the brilliant light of truth to shine through. This transcendental conversion is called Stream-Winning; it is an irreversible state, and the changes in behaviour that it gives rise to are permanent. The Pali Tipitaka, the oldest record of the life and teachings of the Buddha, describes many examples of both mundane and transcendental conversion. Perhaps the most interesting of these is that of the householder Upali (*Majjhima Nikaya*, Discourse 56). He was a disciple of Nigantha Nataputta, known to history as Mahavira, the founder

of Jainism and an older contemporary of the Buddha.
Like many laymen of the time, Upali was well versed in
the tenets of his own religion and took a keen interest in
the religious debates that were such a common feature of
ancient Indian intellectual life. Confident that he would
be able to defend the Jain position, Nataputta sent Upali
to debate with the Buddha. But things did not go as
expected. Eventually, after a long and involved discussion, Upali declared that he wished to take the Three
Refuges, that is, to become one of the Buddha's disciples.

> It is excellent, revered sir, truly excellent.
> Just as one might set upright something that
> has been overturned, reveal what has been
> obscured, show the way to one who has
> gone astray or bring a light into the darkness
> so that those with eyes might see things, so
> too in many ways the Lord has made the
> Dhamma clear. I, revered sir, am going to
> the Lord, the Dhamma and the Sangha for
> refuge. May the Lord accept me as a lay
> disciple going for refuge from today onwards
> for as long as life lasts.

However, rather than accept Upali's avowal of faith, the
Buddha urged him to take time to consider carefully
before making such an important decision.

> Make a proper investigation first. Proper
> investigation is essential in the case of well-
> known people like yourself.

At this time in ancient India there was considerable
competition between the various sects to get disciples,

and Upali was surprised and delighted by the Buddha's unexpected advice.

> I, revered sir, am even more pleased and satisfied with what the Lord says. If the members of other sects had secured me as a disciple, they would have paraded a banner all around Nalanda, saying: "The householder Upali has become our disciple." But the Lord asks me to make proper investigation first.

Once again Upali asked to be accepted as disciple. Seeing that his resolve was strong and that he knew what he was doing, the Buddha finally agreed. However, knowing that the enthusiasm of new converts sometimes makes them hostile towards their former faith, the Buddha suggested that Upali continue to offer the support he had so long given to the Jains.

> Householder, your family has for a long time supported the Jains, so think it right to continue to give them alms when they come.

The Buddha's unpartisan attitude towards other religions was as rare in ancient India as it is today, and it convinced Upali that he was dedicating himself to a teacher who both practised and preached to others openness and undiscriminating generosity.

> I, revered sir, am even more pleased and satisfied with what the Lord says. I have heard that you say: "Gifts should be given to me and my disciples, not to others. What is given to my disciples alone is of great

fruit, not what is given to others." But the
Lord urges me to give to the Jains also.
Indeed, revered sir, I will know the right
time for that.

Thus Upali's conversion on the mundane level was complete. Later he composed one of the earliest devotional hymns in praise of the Buddha and eventually became a Stream-Winner experiencing transcendental conversion.

In many ways, the first stage of Upali's conversion typifies the experience as it is understood in Buddhism. Firstly, neither the Buddha nor any of his disciples sought Upali out to try to convince him of the uniqueness and value of the Dhamma. Proclaiming the Dhamma in the Buddhist sense means making it available to all who wish to inquire about it, and then leaving any decision beyond that to the individual concerned. Using enticement or pressure in an attempt to convert someone is alien to the Buddhist tradition. A person cannot be forced to believe, let alone to understand, any more than a seed can be forced to germinate. If and when conditions are right, it will sprout. Next, Upali's initial interest in the Dhamma was a result of a discussion about principles and ideas - it was more a response of the intellect than the emotions. Conversions that are a response to supposed miracles, or which take place in a highly emotional atmosphere or which come as a catharsis after a long period of mental struggle and turmoil are not the norm in Buddhism, and are looked upon with a certain degree of suspicion. While faith must play some part in any conversion, that faith is best which grows out of an appreciation of the logical consistency of the ideas being considered, their reasonableness and their correspondence with known facts. In one of his discourses, the Buddha mentions some of the things helpful in the discovery of truth - they include weighing things up, testing the meaning and listening carefully (*Majjhima Nikaya*, Discourse 95). To do this, of course, one requires time, and it was for this reason that the Buddha advised Upali to go slowly and consider carefully. Sudden conversions are known in Buddhism, the case of Angulimala the murderer being an example, but more usually they are preceded by a period of study, reflection and consideration. Certainly, such preliminaries are encouraged. The last characteristic of conversion in Buddhism which is illustrated by Upali's story is that strong commitment to the Dhamma does not preclude respect for and cooperation with other religious traditions. On the contrary, it requires it. Upali had long given alms to the Jain ascetics who visited him, and the Buddha encouraged him to continue his generosity even though he had become a Buddhist. Even today, it is common for people in Buddhist countries to lend their support to non-Buddhist religious institutions and to respect the clergy of other faiths. This behaviour is often described as tolerance, but to do so is to miss a very important point. Tolerance is a putting up with, a forbearance towards something or someone whose presence is irritating. Buddhists can respect, even support, other religions not because they can "stand them", but because Buddhism acknowledges that other religions contain many important insights and that they too stress the importance of virtue. Truth, understanding and goodness are rare enough in the world, and they should be rejoiced in and encouraged wherever they are found.

But mundane conversion is only the beginning of the quest for Nirvana. The task of walking the Eightfold Path still lies ahead. It is only by patiently and diligently cultivating the steps on the Path that one will experience the conversion that cannot be reversed.

Encounters with Buddhism

The Anglo-Catalan author Amadeo Sole-Leris was born in Spain in 1927. He graduated in Spanish and German at the University of London, where he subsequently taught Spanish language and literature at King's College. In 1961 he became an international civil servant with the Food and Agriculture Organization of the United Nations (FAO) at its headquarters in Rome. Since retiring from FAO in 1986, he has continued to act as an international conference interpreter on a freelance basis.

How I Became a Buddhist

Amadeo Sole-Leris

The Oxford Dictionary defines religion as: "Recognition on the part of man of some higher unseen power as having control of his destiny, and as being entitled to obedience, reverence and worship." I became a Buddhist as soon as I understood that Buddhism, or to put it more properly, the Dhamma, is not a religion in this sense. Or, indeed, in any sense implying belief in the existence of a supreme, ultimate divinity and seeking the meaning of our existence in our relationship with that divinity.

It was on my second visit to Sri Lanka in 1972 that, thanks to an opportunity to have closer contact with local Buddhists, I began to realise that the teaching of the Buddha could rather more accurately be described, in Western terms, as humanism, that is, as a system of ethical discipline and mental training which (leaving aside metaphysical and theological cogitations as unprofitable) offers everyone a way of life, here and now, which makes it possible to achieve that fullest realisation of human potential described as enlightenment.

When I understood that the Buddha, the Awakened One, never made any claim to be God, or the Son of God, or a prophet revealing God's truth, but was simply the supreme example of what a human being, any human being, can be, I said to myself: "That makes sense - the Awakened One teaches us how to wake ourselves up." But it took time, many years, before I came to realise that this was the case. It took time, because when one

3

starts trying to discover what the Buddha's message actually is, one is faced with a bewildering variety of "interpretations". In the West, the two most common misconceptions (even, all too often, among supposedly qualified scholars) consist in considering the Buddha as teaching either a nihilistic philosophy (*nibbana* as extinction), or else some sort of eternalism (*nibbana* as some kind of paradise), the latter including various theistic variants (the Buddha as God, or as a representative, or manifestation of the Godhead). In the East, the Buddha's original teaching was subjected, in the course of the centuries, to the (historically inevitable) influences of the cultures and religions with which it came into contact as it spread to Southeast Asia, Tibet, China, Korea and Japan, and thus acquired, at least superficially, many intellectual, emotional and ritual accretions which have little in common with the essence of the Dhamma. Moreover, there was, and continues to be, considerable pressure on the part of traditional Hinduism (especially in its Vedantic and Upanishadic forms) to bring back into the orthodox fold this uncomfortably heretic doctrine, which declares even Brahman/Atman an illusion of the unenlightened mind. Thus, even today, one hears it said in India that the Buddha was an avatar of Vishnu, that nirvana (*nibbana*) simply means that realisation of the identity of Brahman and Atman, and so on.

This is why, even though my interest in Eastern thought and culture went back to my early youth (I was studying Patanjali's *Yoga Sutras* - in English translation - at the age of twenty, and from 1949 I practised *Hatha yoga* intensively for over two decades), for many years I went on believing that Buddhism was just a variety of orthodox Hinduism, that is, a way of seeking a mystical union with some kind of World Soul, or of realising the essential identity between one's soul, atman or whatever and a transcendental entity postulated as being unique, eternal and the only reality.

By nature and upbringing I had, and still have, very little inclination to theology and devotionalism. Although born in Spain, a Catholic country, I grew up in an agnostic environment, was never baptised and frequented free-thinking Swiss and English schools and universities. I was fully aware, of course, of the cultural importance of the Christian tradition as a major root of the European civilisation to which I belong, and endeavoured accordingly to inform myself about its tenets, practices, historical achievements and disasters, but I could never accept as literal truth, or even as useful symbology, claims about the uniqueness and superiority of the Christian faith, divine revelation, transubstantiation, and so on. This is why, as a young student, I turned to the East. But there, as I have just indicated, I found myself faced with metaphysical, theological, devotional and ritual claims which were formally different from those in the West but, to me, similarly unconvincing in substance.

From the mid-1950s I travelled a lot, for professional reasons, to many parts of the world including India and the Far East, and took whatever opportunities came my way to enquire further. But time was always short and my professional commitments demanding, so contacts remained superficial, and I went on harbouring the mistaken idea that Buddhism was "just one more religion". Until that trip to Sri Lanka, now sixteen years ago, when I was given an anthology of Buddhist texts, translated from the Pali *suttas*, to read. That was the Venerable Nyanatiloka's *The Word of the Buddha*, a book which, since its first publication in the early years of the century, has become a classic and of which it has rightly been said that "it cannot be estimated how many were introduced to the Buddha's teaching or gained a clear understanding of it through that book."[1] I am certainly among them. On reading those simple, sensible statements, formulated in calm, straightforward language, I was immediately struck by the extraordinary directness and by the pragmatic, concrete character of the Buddha's teaching. In the old words that recur in so many of the Buddha's discourses, it truly was "as though someone had set upright what had been upside down, uncovered what was concealed, shown the way to one who was lost, or carried a lamp into the darkness, that those who have eyes might see."

Along with *The Word of the Buddha*, I was also given a piece of excellent advice - to read the Venerable Nyanaponika's *The Heart of Buddhist Meditation*, another classic of twentieth century Buddhist literature. This proved invaluable in two ways: firstly, by its content, making clear the importance of practice (over and above intellectual understanding) in pursuing the Buddha's way, and specifically the paramount need to train and develop one's mind through the systematic cultivation of right mindfulness; secondly, by its tone and manner - serene, unemphatic yet unambiguous, totally non-confrontational - which exemplified the same qualities of equanimity and loving care that had so struck me on reading the Buddha's words. Here was living proof, even after so many centuries, of the qualities which the Dhamma brings forth in those who live by it. They were abundantly demonstrated subsequently in the correspondence established in response to a first written query from me, and which continues to this day (in addition to later personal contact) as a source of ever-fresh guidance and instruction. I may add that, a few years later, I found these same qualities strikingly exemplified in the *vipassana* meditation master S. N. Goenka, from whom I have learnt whatever skill in meditation I possess.

So this, you might say, was my "conversion". It did not feel particularly dramatic. It was rather a first realisation that here was something eminently worth pursuing, something that offered a sense of direction and real possibilities. It also, clearly, required earnest application. So I got down to it. I took the Three Refuges, and embarked on a comprehensive study of the fundamentals of Dhamma and, in particular, of the Theravada literature. Here I benefited greatly from the Buddhist Publication Society, both from their steady stream of publications and the kindly personal advice of the late Richard Abeyasekera, then Honorary Secretary of the Society, to whose memory I should like to pay tribute here. I also learned Pali (being a linguist by profession, I was especially aware of the importance of reading texts in the original whenever possible) and, from 1975 onwards, started S. N. Goenka's intensive courses in *vipassana* meditation in the lay Burmese tradition of U Ba Khin.[2]

S.N. Goenka's instruction proved extremely enlightening. It was through the practice of insight meditation under his inspiring guidance that I began to live the Dhamma in actual fact, that is, that I took the step from intellectual conviction to living experience. It is the living experience that continues to grow more meaningful with the passing years, and which inspires the other Dhamma activities to which I devote available time: continued study, of course, but also, as opportunities offer, the endeavour to tell others about what the Buddha taught, both in writing (articles, essays, a couple of books) and through lectures and seminars. All this at an elementary, introductory level, speaking as a layman to other lay persons, and especially to those who have no knowledge or - as I myself before - an inaccurate knowledge of the Buddha's teaching, so as to help them realise its vital relevance to all of us today in the East and West and its inestimable benefits here and now.

And these benefits are apparent from the very beginning, provided one does try honestly, without self-deceit and with a minimum of perseverance. From my own still-limited experience I can testify that the practice of insight meditation - the heart of the Buddha's teaching - has done much to develop some positive qualities, such as a better understanding of myself and others, and an attitude of greater openness and balance which - in addition to its intrinsic value - is often helpful in all sorts of everyday situations. And, above all, it has significantly enhanced my peace of mind. Of course, there is still much to be done; much impatience and agitation, especially, to be eliminated. But the results are encouraging. As I sometimes say to my wife when she tells me to calm down: "You don't know how much more agitated I would be if I didn't practise meditation!"

Of course, it is essential to remember at all times that

meditation is not something one practises in a vacuum, at certain specified times, without relation to what one does the rest of the time or how one does it. As I wrote elsewhere, the three main sections of the Noble Eightfold Path, which formulate the Buddha's cure for our sufferings, namely moral discipline, meditative concentration and wisdom "are indissolubly linked together and operate simultaneously. Wisdom cannot be achieved without meditation, but meditation is ineffective (or sometimes downright harmful) if it does not go together with moral discipline. In fact, they are simply three aspects of the same thing: for an Enlightened One, action, meditation and wisdom are one and the same - different modes of an integrated, conflict-free consciousness... Progress takes place through the mutual interaction of all factors: meditation, correctly practised, improves understanding or wisdom - one grows increasingly aware of the impermanent and impersonal nature of everything. This greater awareness has, quite naturally, beneficial effects on one's behaviour. In its turn, the greater purity of behaviour in whatever one does, says and thinks provides a better foundation for meditation. Thus a rising spiral is established in which morality, meditation and wisdom grow ever more complete and better integrated, until the full integration of enlightenment is achieved."[3]

For most of us, the full integration of enlightenment is not exactly round the corner. But since even the most modest efforts towards it, undertaken with proper understanding and care, already produce clearly beneficial effects for oneself and, consequently, for others, there is surely no more sensible and cheering prospect under the sun than the pursuit of the Dhamma.

Notes

1. "Nyanatiloka Mahathera, His Life and Work" by Nyanaponika Thera, in *Nyanatiloka Centenary Volume* (Buddhist Publication Society, Kandy, 1987), p.15.

2. Vipassana International Academy, Dhammagiri, Igatpuri 422 403 (Dist. Nasik), Maharashtra, India. This is the world centre. There are national centres or contacts in Australasia, various Western European countries, the United Kingdom and the USA.

3. *Tranquility and Insight*, by A. Sole-Leris (Century Hutchinson, London, and Shambhala, Boston, 1986), pp.19-20

Linda Brown was born in the United States in 1950 and was educated at Tufts University, where she earned a B.A. magna cum laude *in French and Art History. Later, she received a Masters of Business Administration from the University of California, Berkeley, and was awarded California Marketing Thesis of the Year by the American Marketing Association. She has worked for a major American corporation as a regional merchandise manager in several locations in Asia. At present, Miss Brown works as a business development consultant for a refugee organisation.*

From Corporate America to Refugee Camp

Linda Brown

The search... it's no longer the subtle driving force behind my actions. It was there, so obvious to all who knew me. The search for something more to life, a search for the reason for so many contradictions between our ideals and our actions.

I can't say that the search ended because I found anything. Although Buddhism has been instrumental in helping me put life's discrepancies into perspective, and has given me a method to change the negative thoughts, actions, and habits that were actually the cause of the things I didn't like in life, I cannot say that Buddhism is the treasure at the end of the hunt. Buddhism is much more than a mere precious gem: it is a way of living life.

The search ended because the attitude, and thus activity, of looking for happiness outside myself was transformed into an attitude of accepting something inside of me. I accepted that my own ego, its desires and its dislikes, were the cause of the discrepancies. My expectations of my own behaviour as well as that of others, were the cause of my disappointments and thus my anger. Desire for power, for prominence in the business community, merely a desire of the "I" to be made permanent through recognition, were the causes of the tension I felt from others.

Buddhism has been the tool that carved a gentler, accepting self from the hard, demanding self. It is the tool that is always in my back pocket, and is pulled out frequently to continue the daily reshaping of this mind and its activities.

As a child I was curious about many things. "What will I be when I grow up?" An interest in insects and animals turned into a passion for stars and outer space, transformed into a love of poetry and literature, and grew into a fascination with genetics. Luckily, my parents were quite tolerant of the myriad vacillations, only impressing on my mind that whatever I did, I had to be financially independent. They were disappointed when, upon graduation from a prestigious East Coast university in the U.S., this youngest daughter, the only sibling amongst all the relatives to receive a degree *magna cum laude*, decided to become a travel agent. I was not too excited either, but during an economic recession, even a *magna cum laude* graduate was not considered much in the professional community. My parents taught me I had to be self-supporting, so I swallowed my pride and accepted minimum wage as a travel agent.

After working three years, I had learned and accepted enough about myself to determine that creative skills and research skills could be best blended in a business environment, so I applied to a Masters in Business programme. Two years of hard work under the care of professors stretched every corner of my brain.

I graduated. To my surprise it was again with honours: top in marketing. This time Mom was pleased with the job offers. (Dad had died from cancer before I even considered graduate school.) However, I was a bit wary, as my ego was flying. It would be dangerous to start into a major corporation's fast track programme feeling that I knew everything. So I borrowed money from my brother and went to Indonesia for an undetermined amount of time to cool off.

Living in Flores, a primitive island experiencing a three year drought, brought me back to reality. Eating only tapioca root, hiking through mountainous jungle alone, twice close to death with malaria, once from natives stoning me, I learned the preciousness of life. Empathy towards other living beings, once felt so strongly as a child, returned. Knowing that there were a lot more lessons to be learned, I did not want to leave Indonesia. Yet, with no intellectual stimulation, I knew I would get bored and would not be able to take advantage of such lessons. So I returned to the U.S. and started the corporate life.

With my ego subdued, I got along well with my colleagues and bosses. However, I realised that playing politics well and "being one of the boys" were more important than the skill one showed in making profitable business decisions. Trying to take it positively, I compared the entrance of a female novice into the corporate world to the anthropologist entering the world of a New Guinea tribe: they both must observe the foreign behaviour. Here the comparison ends, as the novice must assimilate the behaviour, whereas the anthropologist studies and writes about it and then leaves. However, as I did not respect the behaviour I saw in the male-dominated corporate world and did not want to emulate it, I could not assimilate into the environment.

The conflict caused such tension, that I went with a friend to Odion, a Tibetan Buddhist retreat centre, to get away and reflect. There I felt peaceful for the first time, and with clarity saw the nonsense of the office situation. Life's conflicts were put into perspective. I felt balanced and light. I ran to tell my friend, who introduced me to Tarthang Tulku, a reincarnate Tibetan lama living in California. He laughed at my realisations, tapped me on the head and said to come back.

Later, I asked my friend about Buddhism. His explanation drew me in more and more. I read some Buddhist books that showed how to take a Buddhist approach to the work situation. The benefits were clear, but it was difficult to practice. And I was unhappy.

A promotion and transfer to Southeast Asia was the break I needed: away from the corporate headquarters' management style and the ever-increasing politics. In the Hong Kong branch of the corporation, I was challenged far more than in the U.S., and although there were politics, being a foreigner, I was outside most of it.

Afraid of being brainwashed by Hong Kong's emphasis on material wealth, I delved into work. Developing relationships, reading, and even playing squash were all extensions of work. When the imbalance was too great, I would do what all Hong Kong people do: shop. Eventually window shopping turned into accumulating expensive antiques, jewels, and clothes. On the verge of buying a mink coat I stopped, looked at myself very carefully and realised that materialism had crept in despite my wish to avoid it. And worse, none of these acquisitions gave me any true happiness.

It was then a little voice started nagging: where will you be ten years from now? What is the importance of selling millions of dollars more of products? What will you really have at the top of the corporate ladder?

I did not like the answers. It was time to review what I had been doing these past ten years, re-evaluate life's goals. Years back, a friend advised that if ever one felt that one's mind was blocked, and one had lost perspective, to take a four-week trek in the Himalayas. The mind would expand like the clear luminous sky above. I resigned and went to Nepal.

The physical exertion of the hike, and the beauty of the scenery did loosen my mind. In this relaxed state I was open to new suggestions. I bought a book, this time on Tibetan Buddhism. I finally felt "at home". Here was a philosophy whose code of ethics was what had been guiding my life. Like a starved person I craved more and more understanding of this new discovery.

I read *The Snow Leopard* which described how a scientist came to Nepal in search of a rare beast, and instead had a spiritual awakening. Like a greedy child I pouted: "Why isn't that happening to me? Why can't I have a spiritual experience?" Little did I know what was just around the corner.

I promised myself that when I returned to Hong Kong, I would not be distracted by the business world, but would look for a Tibetan lama to teach me more. Then I realised there was little chance of finding a Tibetan lama in Hong Kong. I was now in the best place in the world to find one. So off I went.

Down the road was Kopan, a monastery which welcomed Western people interested in Buddhism. A two-week class in meditation had just begun. But it was not taught by a Tibetan lama, it was taught by a Norwegian nun! I wanted the best, and nothing but a Tibetan lama would do. However, someone at the monastery, well-experienced with the snobbism of Westerners, suggested that I just try the course. I agreed to interview the teacher, and if she was good enough I might consider staying.

After waiting an hour (a long time for a Hong Kong executive; didn't these people know the value of time?) I was shown to her room. Inge softly welcomed me and asked how she could help. I went on for at least ten minutes about my experience in the mountains, my realisations and how I had a vision of emptiness. I just wanted to perfect it a bit. Gently Inge responded, "Your expectations are so high, I'm afraid I will disappoint you. Perhaps you should not take the course. You see, I don't feel qualified to teach, as I've only studied twelve years. But my teacher says I must. I spend much time preparing, but I am afraid I won't be able to answer their questions, that I may mislead them. I pray for my teacher to guide me through this."

Never had I ever heard such genuine humility. For someone who had learned both in school and in the business world to sell oneself, to never admit one's inadequacies in comprehension or education, to fake it if one is caught not knowing something, this humility was a shock. I knew that this woman had a lot to teach me and I thought that if I could be an attentive, encouraging student, perhaps she would not be so afraid. So I stayed.

Step by step Inge took us through the Four Noble Truths, and using both meditation and teaching, showed us how to confront ego and all its negative activities. As we practised imagining friends who turned to enemies, strangers to friends, and enemies to friends; as we considered the loving-kindness of our mother and others who have taken the time and care to help us through our childhood; as we explored the physical suffering of others, and our own mental sufferings, layer after layer of this ego was peeled away. At the end I felt lighter, and yet I realised it was only the beginning. There was so much more to uncover inside my heart and mind.

Would I ever have the free time to spend exploring my mind? Was there really a need to go back to Hong Kong? I could always get another job, but would I ever again have the opportunity to take my mind apart and get to the core?

It was time to continue on this journey inward, so I went to Dharamsala, India to start a three-month retreat in silence, and alone.

I had always told myself that by age 35 I would take a break and sail alone around the world. As I went into retreat I realised I was taking that journey. It was a voyage within, an exploration of the deepest, hidden parts of the self. Through retreat, further teachings and pilgrimages to Buddhist sites in India, Nepal and Tibet, that voyage transformed into a cultivation of the mind. In debating the validity of many Buddhist tenets, behaviours from the past were dug up and examined. If they were useful they were replanted, if they were only negative manifestations of an untamed ego, they were chopped up and offered to Buddha. The earth of my mind was turned over again and again until all roots had been pulled up. The soil ready to receive fresh cuttings, I went to teachings and read sutras.

At the end of two years, it was time to test my understanding of Dharma in daily life. Within the confines of a retreat house I was convinced of the benefits of generosity, patience and the other virtues. I understood the importance of compassion, and I was even beginning to comprehend the humble dedication to a teacher who in his wisdom can help guide us past our prejudices, blind spots and weaknesses. But would Dharma still be valid and guide my actions in the world as I knew it before the retreat?

Instead of my activities being for the purpose of gaining money to invest and spend, they could be for the benefit of others less fortunate than myself. By confronting the same situations with a new attitude, I could see how profound the changes of the past two years were.

Looking for a way to begin, I decided to start a home for the unwanted: children, adults, dogs, cats, any living creature. There were so many unwanteds in India.

However, some friends said there was no need for such a home, there were enough orphanages. If instead there was something I could do to help refugees become self-sufficient, that would be of benefit.

So, the past eighteen months of my life have been dedicated to helping Tibetan refugees in India develop small businesses using the talents they brought with them to make products or offer services to the local market. Although my motivation has been to help the refugees, I have found that this work helps me to grow, through integrating Buddhist principles in my working environment and daily life activities.

This work takes me back to America where I can appreciate the kindness and generosity of many Americans to impoverished or sick people. It brings me back to my own society where I must confront again and again the premises I grew up thinking were reality.

The work brings me back to India, to the people who taught me Dharma. With open eyes I see that they are not all perfect practitioners, they are not the Buddha. Some are as selfish and hypocritical as some of the Christians I met as a child.

Within charitable organisations I am confronted with the same actions that were so frustrating in the corporate world. Important decisions are made at a very high level, and one has very little influence over them, although these decisions influence oneself and one's colleagues. People revert to familiar behaviour in times of crises, even though they know that alternate behaviour will bring about a desired result. Valuable time is lost when individuals forget to attend to the details of running a business.

What has it helped me to realise? That again my expectations are too high. There are selfless, kind, generous individuals who follow a Christian path, just as there are similar individuals who follow the Buddhist path. And conversely, both religions have followers who appear to be ignoring the essence of their religion in their daily activities. However, most individuals are doing the best they can with what skills and opportunities they have been given.

With respect to the people I am trying to help, I have to remember to accept where they are in terms of their "professional" development and what learning capabilities they have. I too have had and still have certain blind spots, certain behaviours that prevent me from learning. My teachers are patient, not angry with my ignorant mind, and try to find skilful ways to teach through example and activity. A guru would not have disciples if everyone were perfect.

So I too must think as would a guru: how I can best help these people with what THEY want to accomplish, not what I want them to accomplish.

It is difficult to help others when my own negative habits such as impatience, desiring perfection, and having high expectations return again and again. These I must face daily, and with the compassion of a mother for a learning child, help guide my selfish mind.

Thinking of impermanence and selflessness helps my mind to accept that there are many views of the same situation and thus many possible actions to be based on these varying perspectives. There is no one right way to achieve a goal.

Since organisations are groups of people working toward the same goal, their strengths and weaknesses stem from the strengths and weaknesses of the individuals. Hence if the best way to help others is to compassionately accept their situation, and like a guru teach in a manner that is most appropriate to the individual, then would that not be the best way to also work with and within organisations?

When faced with difficult situations, what good does it do to run away, to resign? The grass is not greener on the other side. It is better to face what is in front of us, and use each situation to transform our own mind. Each situation is an opportunity to practise generosity, patience, wisdom and other perfections. If these are not at the core of our daily activities, then how can we ever hope to be enlightened?

Someone said: "When the going gets tough, the tough get going." Now I see it differently. When the going gets tough, I look at my own ego to determine whether it is myself that is creating the difficulty. That ego, like a nasty little dog, is yap, yap, yapping at my heels. So I must teach it to be still. And if the going gets even tougher, I stop, and reflect on the advice of a Tibetan Rinpoche: it does not matter if you earn your life as a monk or nun, a doctor, teacher or business person. What is important is the attitude with which you do your work, the attitude with which you relate with other sentient beings.

Bhikkhu Amaro was born in England in 1956. He was educated at Bedford College, London University where he earned a joint-honours degree in psychology and physiology. He entered a monastery six months after his graduation.

Journey into Silence

Bhikkhu Amaro

Of all the questions one gets asked, as a Westerner and a Buddhist monk, probably the commonest is: "Why did you become a Buddhist?" In response to this, one has to point out that in truth the question does not apply. This is not just in order to be clever or cryptic, but because, for myself and many others, the experience has not been that of becoming a Buddhist, but rather discovering that one had always looked at life in a 'Buddhist' way. When I was travelling in Thailand and I encountered the Theravada teachings and Buddhist way of life for the first time, the overriding sensation was that of: "How amazing - not only are there other people who think the same way as me, but there is a whole body of teachings which lays it all out far clearer than I ever could hope to do. Not only that, but there is also this monastic tradition, which has flourished over 25 centuries, and a whole culture which celebrates, supports and honours a person's endeavour to give up worldly ambition and actualise the goal of the religious life."

Only a very small number of Westerners seem to express the feeling that they have 'given up' their old faith in order to be a Buddhist; this is particularly so for those interested in Buddhist meditation. It is true that there is often a sense of disaffection, but more importantly the discovery of the Buddha's teaching seems to bring other religious symbolism to life - it makes sense of it and yet at the same time supersedes it. In the simile of the elephant's footprint (which can encompass the footprints of all other creatures) the Buddha described how all other religious teachings can be contained within the Dhamma since it is based on universal Truth, known through the investigation of experience. This certainly was the way it occurred in my life: on encountering the Buddha-Dhamma there was the feeling: "At last it all makes sense" - there was no need to reject other philosophies and religious teachings, as it was clear they were attempting to point towards the same reality. All the confusion and distress which had arisen previously had only been because of having taken symbols too literally, or having been told to believe what it was reasonable to doubt.

The adoption of the Buddhist path rather than that of my native culture was thus not so much a criticism of the latter, but more the inclination to use that which was to hand and in which faith had arisen. I felt as though I had been wandering helplessly down a desert road and then up had swept an air-conditioned bus, which not only stopped and offered to take me where I wanted to go, but was also filled with the most pleasant people with whom to share the journey. To take their assurance that they were headed for 'The Heavenly City' and that to arrive there was a possibility, and then to say: "Thanks for the offer but your bus is the wrong colour," seemed like madness to me. This was the situation I had found myself in - I could not imagine finding more noble people, a more simple life or more direct guidance on the spiritual path. "These are my people," I realised, and so I stayed.

It is no exaggeration to say that not everybody at the age of twenty-one gleefully leaps into the "holy life" as soon as the opportunity is presented, with nary a backward glance. In the first flush of one's enthusiasm one is astonished, in fact, to see so many people make contact with Buddhist teachings and pass on through unchanged. It becomes clear that realising the Truth is not the most urgent priority for everyone - people experienced what was apparently the same situation, and I began to consider how it had come about that I saw things the way I did - what had brought to me such certainty that this was the right path. On looking back over the memories of my life some very distinct patterns began to emerge....

I was born in England, in the county of Kent, on September 2nd, 1956. My parents were from a middle-class background, and at the time they supported the family by farming. There was little religious influence in my early life, as both parents had become disillusioned with Christianity at an early age and were not church-going people. The schools I went to were also technically Christian, but I experienced an almost constant dissatisfaction with the religion as it was presented: I had an inquiring mind which was not content with simply believing what I was told. Questions would often come to mind, and those around me plainly did not really know the answers. There was a feeling of being given the 'party line' rather than hearing what came from direct knowledge.

My parents were not wealthy, but because of a scholarship I was able to attend a 'public' school. I found it quite easy academically but, as time went by, it became increasingly difficult to adhere to the educational system. There was a lot of teasing and bullying which, allied with the general trauma of early teens, made the whole experience into something of a nightmare. I did my best to survive and make the most of it, but in the course of time I became quite a difficult pupil: talented in the classroom and on the sports field, but a rebel and un-disciplined in conduct.

During this time my religious sense was developing but it stayed very much underground. I could not align the Christianity I saw with my own intuition of what was ultimately real; also, amongst the company I kept, reli-gion was definitely out. I knew in my heart that there was something beyond this sensory world, and that somehow perfect freedom was possible. I realised that freedom was what religion must be talking about, but the only way I found to experience it at this time was through partying and different types of intoxication.

Aged seventeen now, I left home and entered higher education the following autumn. I went to Bedford College, University of London, reading a joint-degree in psychology and physiology. My interest in spirituality began to grow more rapidly at this time and I started to attend regular talks given by a man from the Rudolf Steiner tradition. Over the weeks and months a vast array of subjects was covered - fascinating intricacies of cosmology and metaphysics, the workings of the wheels of kamma, the history of European spirituality, the celestial hierarchies and hidden worlds - it was all wonderful stuff to listen to. To follow up its implications, however, to actually do something about the way I lived my life - that was another story. I seemed to be so busy producing essays, trying to pass exams and hanging out with my friends that yoga and meditation were seen as something I would get around to once some free time appeared. It was true that I felt there was something missing in my life, but at that point, I assumed the absent 'thing' was the next thrill rather than the peaceful heart.

Curiously enough, during this whole period, I never read any Buddhist books; my interest was always diverted by more gratifying and spectacular teachings, usually those which were quirky, inspirational or of a monastic inclination - God as the fabric and essence of all things, The Great Spirit, or Brahman, immanent eternal Unity. Despite the presence of such high-minded philosophies in my thoughts, in order to stave off a growing sense of anguish and insecurity, the descent into hedonism gathered pace. However, despite the narrowing gap between the experience of angst and the escape into oblivion, something in me knew I had to undertake the spiritual path - how and where and in what form though, I did not know.

In 1977 I received my Bachelor's Degree and, as I had the chance of a free flight as a groom for racehorses on a cargo plane to Malaysia, I decided to travel to the East. My twenty-first birthday fell in September of that year, so I threw a final party to which I invited everyone I knew, said my good-byes and left on a one-way ticket. As I travelled through Southeast Asia, trying to visit mystical places, I found to my horror that all the hang-ups and problems I had hoped to leave behind in England seemed to have jumped on the plane and come with me. When I left I had undertaken to give up drinking and smoking and had determined to become a vegetarian. Constantly, however, as I went from place to place, I found myself amongst the same kind of crowd I had left behind. I knew I needed to get away.

I left the group of people I had been living with on a beach in the south of Thailand and set off on my own to the remote northeastern provinces. I had been given the address of some English doctors who worked at a refugee camp and, taking their house as a starting-off point, arrived there in early January 1978. It transpired that the doctors I had the contact with were away at that time, so not wishing to impose, I asked about other places to visit nearby. One of the nurses told me of a Buddhist monastery of Western monks which they had just visited over Christmas, and from what she said, it seemed that I might be able to stay there a few days. "That should be interesting," I thought, and I was right - those few days have now stretched to fill ten years.

This was the International Forest Monastery which had been set up under the guidance of the Ven. Sumedho two years before. What I found there seemed to be the answer to all my aspirations: a group of cheerful and good-hearted people living an austere and simple life dedicated to the realisation of the Truth. No charges were made; nothing more was asked of one than to follow the daily routine and honour the monastic discipline. The principle was that the only usefulness in being there was in participation as a member of the community; just to hang around and take a look was of no benefit. I was joyous at this wonderful find, and felt as though some great hand had plucked me up off the beach and had dropped me in this forest - now all I had to do was get on with it.

The odds and ends of religious teachings and philosophies I had played with over the years suddenly all fell into place. The Buddha-Dhamma illuminated it so clearly: the fundamental problem, its cause and the way beyond - there was no doubt in my mind that I had found the path. On the third day I was there I shaved my head and three weeks later took the Eight Precepts formally. I was given the samanera precepts in July of 1978 and the bhikkhu ordination in April of 1979; the Ven. Ajahn Chah was my preceptor as he was still in good health at that time.

I suppose that right from that first contact until now, the most constantly appealing and refreshing aspect of the Buddhist Way has been its non-dogmatic spirit: one is encouraged to doubt, to inquire, to investigate profoundly and learn from one's experience of life. The presentation of the scriptural teachings also echoes this - we do not hear the Buddha proclaiming the Absolute Truth for us to believe in, but we hear Elder Ananda saying: "Thus have I heard." The encouragement is for us to reflect upon the word of the Buddha rather than to blindly adhere to our interpretation of it, no matter how sure we may be that we are right.

The other key element of the Buddhist path, which seems more and more important as time goes by, is that of simplicity. At first I often felt that the teaching was a bit impoverished; it seemed a little stingy that the Buddha only offered us a "a handful of leaves". Over the last ten years, however, I have grown to appreciate the Buddha's unwavering resoluteness in teaching only "suffering and the way beyond suffering". The ability of the mind to become side-tracked by secondary concerns, abstruse speculations and the urgencies of daily living, seems only to be surpassed by its capacity for believing in it all as totally real. With meditation the sense of the enormity of life's mystery develops along with a sense of awe and wonderment; it becomes apparent that there is indeed an infinity of things which can be known, and that to try and grasp it all with the faculties of thought and memory is a futile and unnecessary task. When the mind is free from attachment, there is no struggle to 'solve' the mystery, the clear seeing of it is, in fact, its consummation. The Dhamma thus dwells only upon the most essential points of this vast subject in order to achieve a single purpose: to indicate the habit of attachment and to enable the resultant experience of suffering to end. It simply offers this opportunity: "If this is important to you, then this is all you need to know."

In living for ten years as a Buddhist monk - keeping a strict observance of the Vinaya discipline and spending long periods of the day in formal meditation, it is quite natural to experience profound changes in the way life is perceived; in fact, to not experience such changes would negate the worthiness of the Buddhist path. However, on contemplating what has been most significant, the unfolding of the sense of selflessness constantly reappears as the central theme. There is an ever-growing feeling of relief that all that is perceived, cognised, remembered and created is not 'me', not 'mine', that there is no 'self' in any of this, that the 'person' is actually what is perceived rather than being the perceiver. There is also a sense of freedom from being stretched upon the rack of time, the joints and tendons of the self-image being popped and snapped by the pulls of memory and expectation. As the sense of self fades, the illusion of time goes with it and the mind can rest alert and sensitive to the here and now.

The tendency to create complication and anxiety out of the vicissitudes of life also fades when these worldly dhammas are no longer taken personally. All that is habitually identified with as my crimes and virtues, plus all that is wrong with the world - these are recognised simply to be part of the natural pattern of the conditioned realm. Those qualities that lead to good are followed, those that lead to harm are abandoned, and as we learn from our mistakes, the heart is purified. It becomes apparent that life is very simple when we do not complicate it - there is no need to turn it all into a problem.

John D. Ireland was born in England in 1932. He was educated at Orange Hill Grammar School and works as a Medical Laboratory Scientific Officer. Mr. Ireland has contributed numerous articles to Buddhist journals and is currently preparing a translation of two Buddhist scriptures, the Udana *and the* Itivuttaka.

An Inner Biography

John D. Ireland

I am told I was baptised a Christian, but as I was only a month or so old at the time, I was too young to be able to recollect anything of it. Beyond doing this for me, my parents never gave me any religious instruction. They were nominally Christian and Church of England, but I never knew them to go to church or attend a service, except for the occasional wedding or funeral which was more a social event than anything else. In this they were like the majority of people in our London suburban society. If questioned, they would perhaps have admitted to a somewhat vague belief in 'God' and the 'Bible', but these things were quite irrelevant to their daily lives. If someone evinced a more than passing interest in religion, they were looked on rather askance and as perhaps not quite 'normal'. This was a general attitude prevalent in our English society then and now. Thus, when a child, I was never prompted to go to church or to take any interest in such activities.

My first contact with religion was when I went to school. At morning assembly we had to sing a hymn and learn to recite the 'Lord's Prayer', and then there was a class where we learnt stories from the Bible and read verses from it. This was at the Junior School. I found it all rather meaningless and puzzling. Of course I understood how morality was a good thing, how stealing and telling lies were antisocial behaviour that set one at odds with one's friends and companions. But other things, like the miracles for instance, I could not understand. They seemed

35

unnatural and against the order of how things worked in the world. I doubted the very existence of God as he was presented, and the creation story did not fit in with what I was beginning to learn about science from the reading of books. If there was one thing I learnt very quickly at school, it was to read, and I read everything I could lay my hands·on. This love of reading and books has stayed with me all my life.

One day at the Junior School the headmaster told us a little anecdote 'proving the existence of God' - so he must have known there was room for doubt. He said he carefully planted flower seeds in his garden, yet often they never even sprouted, while weeds would grow and flourish between cracks in the paving and on stony ground. This showed the hand of God at work, helping even the humble weed to grow. I remember thinking about this and concluding that it proved nothing at all about God. If some seeds flourished and others did not, it was merely because the seeds were sound or otherwise, and the conditions for growth were right or not. I then thought further about the whole problem of God and came to the conclusion that God did not exist at all - he was merely a figment of the imagination. I was eight years old at this time. It is interesting that my thoughts on the causes and conditions necessary for a seed to sprout came very close to the Buddha's teaching on causation, but I was only to discover this many years later.

When I left the Junior School and went on to a Grammar School, I learnt more about Christianity, and in fact, passed an examination with good marks in Religious Knowledge. However, it had no special significance for me; it was just another subject to study like any other. In this, I was no different from the rest of my classmates. In those days, up until 1949 when I left school, we were taught nothing about religions other than Christianity, so I hardly knew that alternative religions like Buddhism even existed. Of course there were Jewish boys at my schools, but Judaism seemed not much different from Christianity. They studied the Old Testament only and did not believe in Jesus. Religion was about God, who did not exist for me. Nowadays, I am given to understand, children are taught about other religions and not merely indoctrinated with Christianity.

Although I was not interested in religion as it was presented, I did feel an emotional need for something to believe in. I thought, through being interested in science and natural history in particular, I would devise my own religion. I would cultivate a reverence for nature and worship trees and rivers and the wonders and beauties of nature, as our heathen ancestors did, before the advent of Christianity, I being a heathen too. I sensed there were things that could not be explained by science, something supernatural in the natural world, perhaps. This was reinforced by a strange and inexplicable occurrence when I was about twelve years old. I was walking one day through a wood near my home when there came into my mind the thought that at the foot of a certain tree a little distance away there was a half-a-crown, a silver coin worth more than I received for pocket money in a month at that time. I saw it with my mind's eye, slightly worn and stained yellow with the earth. So convincing and impelling was this idea that I stepped off the path, went round the tree, scraped away the fallen leaves and found the coin, exactly as I had 'seen' it in my mind, worn and marked with yellowish stains. This experience astonished and frightened me, and I remember clutching the coin tightly in my hand, in case it should disappear as inexplicably as it had appeared. I went and spent it straight away, buying something to eat on my way home.

I have described this strange event, not only because it made such a vivid impression upon me - how could it fail to? - but because it had some similarity to a later event, my conversion to Buddhism, another very vivid experience which I describe presently.

I was very happy at school and enjoyed the companionship of friends as well as studies. I would have liked to have continued and perhaps gone on to university, but this was not to be. My parents were not well off and my father was not in good health - the legacy of what he had undergone as a soldier in the 1914-18 war. So I had to go out to work and earn money to help my parents. This was a disappointing period for me. It seemed as if I were thrown suddenly into an adult world ill-prepared, and I missed my school companions. I could not decide what I wanted to do with my life, what career would appeal to me. It was a very frustrating period and I could see no purpose and meaning to life. The future seemed dark and uncertain. Perhaps this is a common experience of many teenagers, and I certainly felt this depression and dissatisfaction very much, and did not know what to do about it.

In the summer of 1951 I was on holiday from work and feeling rather bored. I could not go away on vacation because my father was ill again, and in any case I did not have enough money to go away, even if I felt so inclined. So I just employed my time reading books, doing household chores, or wandering aimlessly around the streets. We did not know it at the time, but this was to be my father's last illness. He was gradually dying, although he lingered on for another two years before eventually passing away. Naturally I was worried about my father, and this increased my gloom and despondency.

One day, during this holiday, I happened to walk into a bookshop with the idea of finding something to read that would relieve my boredom and take my mind away from my problems and worries. And there I chanced upon a paperback book called *Buddhism* by Christmas Humphreys. Up until then, as I have already indicated, I knew nothing at all about Buddhism. I did know in a vague sort of way that it was an Oriental religion, but thought the Buddha was a Chinese god. On seeing this book it occurred to me it might be interesting to find out something about it, if only to help me forget my own troubles for a while. And so, on a sudden impulse, I purchased it.

The next day I started to read it and thought it quite interesting. I learnt about the life of the Buddha, his birth as an Indian prince and about his attainment of Enlightenment and so forth. And then, when I had still not read very far into the book, I came across the description of the Four Noble Truths: the Noble Truth of Suffering, its Origin in Craving, its Cessation and the Noble Eightfold Path. I was absorbed in reading this when it happened. I related the Buddha's statement about suffering, *dukkha*, to my own experiences at that time of worries and troubles and my thoughts on the futility of life. I suddenly understood the Truth of *Dukkha* and said to myself, "This is true, this is the truth!" I was elated by this discovery and had a vision as if I were suspended in space with the earth spread out below me like a map, with India in the centre and people moving about like ants. It was very vivid and detailed and I remember in particular noticing a man walking slowly and wearily beside an ox-drawn cart. Why I especially noticed this or what its significance was, if any, I do not know. While I looked down on this visionary scene I was saying to myself, "All this is suffering caused by craving."

I came out of this state, which had perhaps lasted but a short moment of time, to find myself sitting in my room with the book in my hand feeling intensely happy and excited. As I reflected upon it, the words came spontaneously to me as a solemn statement of fact, "I am now a Buddhist, I have always been a Buddhist and always will be a Buddhist," meaning that as the Buddha had taught this truth which I knew to be a statement of fact verified from my own experience, he must have known it too. The words were the expression of the great faith and respect which I felt for the Buddha who had now become my teacher. There was a subtle timeless quality of the experience. Saying I had always been a Buddhist meant that I had always known the fact of suffering although had not been clearly conscious of it previously. It was something that had always existed, but I had thought rather selfishly of it as only applying to myself. Previously, other people seemed quite happy and contented with life, and it seemed it was me who was out of step with the rest of mankind. But I now knew it to be a universal truth, true for everyone, even if others did not recognise the fact. How I knew that I would always be a Buddhist was a matter of faith and conviction that the Truth of Suffering would not go away. The elation at my discovery was however tinged with disappointment. I accepted the Buddha's statement that the source of suffering lies in cravings and desires, but I had not penetrated the fact in the same way as I had with suffering itself. Although I did attempt to, the moment of vision had gone. Thus, I understood there was more to be done and to learn, and proceeded to find out more about Buddhism as soon as I could.

I continued by reading further and widely on the subject and attempted to discover more about it in other ways. I learnt that there was the Buddhist Society founded by Christmas Humphreys which had its premises at that time near the British Museum in London. A week or so later, I went to look for it during my lunch-break and eventually attended the first of several public meetings there and met other Buddhists. I recollect the very first talk I went to was given by Mr. William Purfurst and was on the Vinaya, the discipline and rules of the Buddhist monk and nun or bhikkhu. Three years later I was to meet him when he had become the Bhikkhu Kapilavaddho. But before this could happen I had to undergo a new variety of suffering in the guise of two years of National Service in the army, which curtailed my studies for a while.

As soon as I was released from the army, I became a member of the Buddhist Society and was introduced by an acquaintance to Bhikkhu Kapilavaddho. He was the first Buddhist monk I met and the first from whom I received the Refuges and Precepts. Now I had formally become a Buddhist. A little later I attended a number of lectures given by him and began to study in earnest the discourses of the Buddha in the Pali Canon in order to learn the basic teachings of Buddhism. Bhikkhu Kapilavaddho was inspiring and energetic in dispelling many misconceptions that were prevalent about Buddhism in those days. I gravitated towards him because what he taught corresponded more closely with what I had discovered and experienced for myself. He also introduced me to the basic practice of mindfulness, and the Buddha's teaching of causality and dependent arising, these two being the fundamentals of practice and understanding.

Later I met other bhikkhus and teachers, besides those of the Theravada tradition. I received valuable instruction and teachings from the late Trungpa Rinpoche, the famous lama of the Kagyud school of Tibet, who was living in Britain before moving to the United States. However, I have continued to study the Buddha's teachings to be found in the Pali Tipitaka, and have taught myself something of the Pali language so that I can read it in the original. Formerly I belonged to several Buddhist organisations, besides the Buddhist Society, and met many fellow Buddhists. But nowadays I have tended to pursue a solitary course, practising, studying and translating, depending on my own inner resources, not meeting many other Buddhists and belonging to no Buddhist organisation. I never married, and now that both my parents are dead, I have no close family ties, so am free to devote my energies to that only worthwhile pursuit - the realisation of the Buddha's teaching.

How has Buddhism changed my life? This is a difficult question to answer. That first experience of my encounter with Buddhism dispelled my depression at that time and also cured my tendency to be bad-tempered. My discovery gave me an inner core of happiness and confidence and a purpose in life which has never left me since that day. What I would be now if I had not become a Buddhist is futile to speculate about.

That moment of my conversion seemed remarkable and astonishing to me at the time, but looking back on it now with the knowledge I have gained since then, it seems even more remarkable. I can hardly believe how fortunate I am to have experienced it. I have recorded two instances when I spontaneously entered a state of *samadhi*, absorbed concentration. When I found the coin was the first, in which was also displayed the effortless exercise of *iddhi*, magical power born of concentration. The second was at the moment of my conversion when I can even recollect the 'factors of absorption' being present: one-pointedness of mind, intent upon a single thought, sustained interest, elation and joy. As these things arise only after prolonged effort in meditation, I think it possible I must have done this work in a previous life and reaped the reward of such meritorious actions in this. While Christianity always appeared something alien and foreign to me, when I discovered Buddhism it seemed a most natural thing, as if I had 'come home again'. So I believe I must have been a follower of the Buddha in a previous life, though I have no memory of it. The Buddha said, "He who sees Dhamma (Truth) sees me, and he who sees me sees Dhamma." And that brief glimpse of Dhamma, when I saw into the nature of suffering, dissatisfaction, was as if I had met the Buddha face to face and received teaching directly from him. The book I was reading, although the instigator of the experience, was irrelevant and unimportant. The implicit trust and confidence in the Buddha that arose at that time has sustained and guided me in so many ways. Without it I would, perhaps, have been like many people I have met, who have followed the practice of Buddhism for a time and then turned to other things. Or I would have been like those who trusted a human teacher and then turned away on discovering he had faults and was not infallible as they had thought. But I have never yet met a teacher whom I would uncritically accept. I have found the only infallible guide is the life and sayings of the Buddha himself. Of course, I have learnt much from others, but listening to what they have to say I measure their words and consider, like Queen Mallika, "Did the Lord say that?" Or, would he have said that? And then, "If the Lord Buddha said this, it must be so."

This briefly, is my 'inner biography', some of those events and thoughts that have impressed themselves on my life and made me call myself a Buddhist.

Venerable Sangye Khadro (Kathleen McDonald) was born in the United States in 1952 and was educated at the University of California at Davis. She received her lower ordination at Kopan Monastery, Nepal, in 1974 and her higher ordination at Hsi Lai Temple in Los Angeles in 1988. Venerable Sangye has taught Buddhism in Europe, America and Australia, and is the author of the popular book How to Meditate.

Happy to be a Nun

Ven. Sangye Khadro

I was born in Sacramento, California, in 1952. Like many Americans, my ancestry is mixed: Scottish-Irish-Dutch on my father's side and German-French on my mother's. My father was born in Iowa, and experienced some hardships in his life. He was eighteen when his father died, around the time of the Great Depression, so instead of attending college he had to work to support his mother and two younger sisters. He moved to Los Angeles in 1936 where he found work and studied in night school to complete his education. In the early 1940's he contracted tuberculosis and spent nearly two years in hospital.

Mother's life was easier: an only child, she was born in Illinois, but her family moved to Los Angeles when she was three. She studied music, and was playing in an orchestra at the time she met my father. After they married, my parents moved to Sacramento where my father began working as an accountant and my mother began to have babies. They had five children, three boys and two girls. I am the second child.

Both of my parents are devout Catholics, and all of us children were educated in Catholic schools. Mother and father were quite strict with us, regulating the amount of time we could play and watch TV, and making sure we always completed our homework. We were not wealthy (school tuition ate up quite a chunk of father's paychecks), but all our basic needs were looked after.

Religion was very much a part of our lives. The whole family attended Mass on Sundays and religious holidays, and the older children went with father to church for confession on Saturdays. This involves telling your sins in private to a priest, who then gives you advice on how to improve yourself. Father sometimes attended weekend retreats at a monastery, where the participants were guided in spiritual prayer and contemplation.

When I was young I had a natural sense of devotion for God, the saints, and the religious teachings I learned at school. Mass was a moving experience: the priest performing the ritual in his beautiful robes, the chanting of prayers in ancient Latin, the choir and organ filling the church with songs in praise of God, the offerings of candles, flowers and incense - it all brought the heart closer to God.

One of the saints, St. Therese of Lisieux, was my child-hood idol. Born in France in the last century, she was saintly as a child, became a nun at the age of fourteen, and died when she was only twenty-two. Her life was a model of dedication to God and religious practice - she was humble, generous, patient, unselfish and always mindful of God. I wanted to be like her and even sometimes thought of becoming a nun, but I didn't seem to have the right qualities. I was impatient and irritable, selfish and greedy. I fought with my brothers and sisters and got angry at my parents when I didn't get what I wanted. I did not want to be like this, but couldn't help it - I was born with a bad temperament, and didn't know how to change. As I grew older, I became more and more frus-trated about not being the person I wanted to be. According to the Catholic teachings, saints are special people, blessed by God with wonderful qualities and abilities - it is not something we humans have any control over. We were told to be good, generous, kind to others, devoted to God and respectful to our parents and teachers, but we were not told how to develop these attitudes if they were lacking. I prayed to God for help, but did not notice any improvement. So as time went on, my religious faith declined, and was replaced by a growing sense of frustration and confusion.

I enjoyed going to school. My favourite subjects were English literature and composition, art, geography and history. I was not interested in sports, but preferred reading in my spare time. Books were magic gateways to other times, other lands, other ways of life. It was through books that I came into contact with Eastern philosophy, and I found the ideas of Buddhism and Hinduism more compatible with my own ways of thinking. At one point I became fascinated with Tibet, and read everything I could find about that country. I began to long for the day when I could actually travel to Tibet, India and the other countries I could then only read about.

The four years of high school were the most difficult of my life. This was the late 1960's, a difficult period for America. The government was bogged down in the Vietnam war, while at home people in the thousands marched in the streets to protest. The long-repressed black population demonstrated to demand their rights, and disillusioned young people flocked to San Francisco in search of peace, love and psychedelic experiences. The voices of the protestors and the lyrics of the songs popular at the time echoed the questions and doubts that were running through my own mind: Why was there war? Why were some people unjust, even cruel, to fellow human beings because of differences in colour, religion, ethnic background or sex? Is there really someone called "God"? If he does exist, why doesn't he do something about the suffering in the world? Why are we here in the first place? And what happens to us after we die?

I felt that the "system" - government, Church, society and educational institutions - was not only unable to provide satisfying answers to such questions, but sometimes contributed to the problems in the world. So, I wondered, who could you trust? I marvelled that most of my classmates were able to absorb themselves in such concerns as clothes, boyfriends, parties and football games, seemingly oblivious to the current troubles. I found only one or two friends who felt the way I did, so I was often lonely and unhappy.

After high school I attended the University of California, Davis campus, not far from home. My declared major was French, but I did not have a clear idea about what I wanted to do in life. I also took classes in other departments such as psychology, anthropology, art and music.

But it was the extra-curricular activities and encounters that made my time at university meaningful. I found many people who, like me, were concerned about world peace and human rights, and some were also interested in spiritual matters. I learned Hatha Yoga and meditation from an Indian teacher, and became friends with a woman who practiced Zen meditation. She was the first Buddhist

I encountered, and helped me to understand better the Four Noble Truths. I began to see that the global and social problems I was concerned about stemmed from greed, hatred, selfishness, intolerance and, at a deeper level, from people not understanding themselves and the nature of existence. As the Buddha and the other masters from the East explained how all these problems could be overcome, I became even more interested in travelling to the source of their wisdom. In the meantime, at university, I continued to learn from books and discussions with my friends.

During my second year, however, my interest in Eastern religion became stronger than my interest in university studies. I began to feel attracted to a life of spiritual contemplation, both as a way to improve myself and find happiness, and as a way to contribute to peace in the world. I felt that I needed a spiritual teacher to guide me, so I decided to leave school and travel to India in search of one. My parents, surprisingly, accepted my decision. Their attitude towards their children is that each one has their own life to live, so they do not interfere in our decisions. They knew I had been unhappy for a long time and was searching for something, and they wished me luck in finding it. Still, they were sad to see me go and worried about what might happen to me.

In October, 1972, I set out with a one-way ticket to London (as I didn't know when I'd be back). I spent the first seven months visiting Europe and North Africa, then another three months travelling overland to India. Although I began my journey alone, I usually travelled with other young "back-packers" I met in youth hostels along the way. To ease my parents' worries, I wrote to them regularly and shared my adventures with them.

My first contact with Buddhist culture was in Bamiyan, a valley in the middle of Afghanistan, where Buddhism had flourished many centuries ago and where one can still see magnificent images of the Buddha carved in the mountainside. Here, visiting caves once inhabited by monks, I met two Australians who had just come from India and told me about Dharamsala, where the Dalai Lama and a number of Tibetan refugees had settled. My old interest in Tibet re-stimulated, I decided to go there. Located in north-west India, it was an easy one-day bus ride from the India-Pakistan border.

Dharamsala is a small town in the foothills of the Himalaya, a place of breathtaking beauty, with snowy peaks rising behind and the vast plains of India spread out below. Here the Tibetan refugees have built a modest "palace" for their spiritual leader, the Dalai Lama, as well as several monasteries, centres for the study and practice of traditional healing arts, carpet factories, a Children's Village - home and school for several thousand Tibetan children - and the Library of Tibetan Works and Archives, where classes in Buddhist teachings are offered in English.

I began attending classes at the Library and was immediately struck by the simple but profound truths of such teachings as impermanence, suffering and the need to develop detachment from the world and pure love for all beings. Other points were more difficult to grasp: the nature of the mind, the possibility of every being attaining enlightenment, selflessness - but nonetheless I found these ideas agreeable and inspiring.

The teachings were inspiring, and so were the teachers. Ven. Geshe Ngawang Dhargyey, who taught the classes, and other Lamas I met displayed unselfishness, sincerity, strength of mind and character, loving-concern for their students, wisdom and humility - qualities I had found lacking in my American teachers. Even the ordinary Tibetan people, in spite of the hardships they had been through, were generally cheerful, generous, gentle and compassionate. In my visits to other countries, I was often disappointed to find that people didn't live in accordance with their religious beliefs. It was therefore refreshing to see the Buddha's teachings practiced in daily life by the Tibetans.

I stayed in Dharamsala for five months, attending classes, reading Dharma books and discussing the teachings with fellow Western students. On one occasion I was fortunate to meet the Dalai Lama: a wonderful experience that sealed my connection with Tibetan Buddhism.

Then, as my permit to stay in India was about to expire, I travelled to Nepal, where study with Tibetan Lamas was also possible. I attended my first month-long meditation course at Kopan Monastery conducted by the Ven. Lamas Zopa Rinpoche and Thubten Yeshe in the spring of 1974. This course is an intensive immersion into Buddha's teachings on the path to enlightenment; the schedule of lectures, guided meditations and discussion runs from 5.00 am to 9.00 pm each day. Instruction in meditation had not been available at the Library in Dharamsala; I had tried it out on my own several times but without much success. So it was at Kopan that I learned to meditate and finally discovered how to work on my mind, how to change negative states of mind into productive, positive ones, methods I had been looking for all my life.

By the end of the course, I had a strong feeling that there was nothing more worthwhile in life than striving to reach enlightenment for the welfare of all beings. It seemed that the renounced way of life was most conducive for this work, so I requested the Lamas to ordain. They agreed, provided my parents gave their consent. For many months I had been writing excitedly to my parents about my encounters with Buddhism and Buddhist monks and nuns, so they were not completely surprised by my wish to become a nun, and again they accepted my decision, saying that whatever I did with my life was fine with them, as long as I was happy.

In May, 1974 I ordained and joined the community of sixty Tibetan and twenty Western monks and nuns at Kopan Monastery. The Westerners had a separate daily programme that included meditation, prayer, study and work. The three months of the rainy season were devoted to intensive meditation retreats, alone or in a group. I stayed in the Kopan community for three years, then returned to America to visit my family. Since then I have lived in different Buddhist communities both in Asia and in Western countries, continuing to develop my understanding and practice of the Buddha's teachings, as well as helping with the running of Buddhist centres, teaching new students and helping to publish English-language material on Buddhism.

So now, sixteen years after first encountering the living tradition of Buddhism, what have I learned? For me, the most precious gifts the Buddha left for us are meditation-methods for transforming the mind: subduing and eventually eliminating the disturbing states of mind such as anger, greed and selfishness, and cultivating positive qualities such as loving-kindness, generosity, and wisdom. I have tried these methods and have found them to be effective. Although I have only just begun to follow the path to enlightenment, I find that I am less angry than before and more happy, peaceful and attentive to others. So I have confidence that if I continue to practice and work on myself, I will develop even further.

Buddhism has also helped me to overcome the anger I used to feel for my native country, religion, and family. I have learned to appreciate the good in everyone and every institution, rather than seeing only faults. Buddhism teaches us that we must recognize and purify our *own* faults, and that when our minds are fault-free, we will see everything and everyone as pure. By putting this idea into practice, I find that my relationships with my parents and others improve all the time.

Buddhism is as relevant today as it was 2,500 years ago. Modern science and psychology are arriving at many of the same ideas that the Buddha taught, based on his direct experience. The Buddha's emphasis on solving human problems from the inside - that is, the mind - is finding acceptance among an increasing number of rational-thinking Westerners. The Buddha's injunction to analyze and put to the test any religious ideas before accepting them is agreeable to those who are suspicious of dogma.

The Buddha's message of non-violence and respect for all life is an important contribution to the efforts to save our planet from destruction. Finally, his teachings on meditation practice provide a source of mental and physical well-being and happiness to many people.

I hope and pray that my life and the work I am doing will contribute to the preservation of the Buddhadharma, and will bring benefit to others. May all beings be happy, free of all suffering, and may they quickly reach enlightenment!

Viqar Zaman was born in India in 1931 and educated in Pakistan and England. At present he is Chairman and Professor of the Department of Microbiology in the National University of Singapore. Professor Zaman is the author of five books, and is a Fellow of the Royal Society of Pathologists and also of the Royal Society of Tropical Medicine and Hygiene.

The Appeal of the Dhamma

Viqar Zaman

I was born into a Muslim family in Hyderabad in central India at a time when the Indian independence movement was gaining momentum. There was great optimism in the air, and people felt that the imminent departure of the British would bring an end to all their suffering and a new India would be born. My generation was highly politicised, and even at the tender age of seven I would join demonstrations and shout slogans. In fact, it was at this age that I had my first experience of tear gas.

In my ancestral home, I had access to a good library which included books on most religions, but in particular on Islam. I read them with great interest, and one day I suggested to my father that I go away to the jungle on a spiritual quest. My father responded with a great deal of understanding and said that I should think about it after I had grown up. But it was not to be.

With partition in 1947 came unimaginable religious conflict, and all our dreams turned into a bloody nightmare. After we moved to Pakistan as refugees, my family was economically ruined and it took me years to rationalise the suddenness with which people who had lived together as neighbours for generations could turn into deadly enemies. Being at an impressionable age, the psychological trauma of all these events was great. I turned away from religion, a change that surprised and sorrowed my parents. I had come to believe that only a radical political change could mend the poverty, injustice and religion divisions that plagued the Indian sub-continent.

I was now a young man about to become a doctor, and although I was totally convinced that religion could never bring peace to India, absolutely certain that I would never to be involved in any organised religion, there was a spiritual yearning within me that I could neither explain nor satisfy. While I was in Scotland doing my post-graduate studies, the liberal environment which I enjoyed very much, allowed me to immerse myself in lively discussions on religion and politics in the various student groups which I joined.

I came into contact with a professor who was Chairman of the Department of Psychological Medicine and a great exponent of hypnosis. I saw and experienced hypnotic phenomena which I found and still find totally fascinating. This interest in hypnosis led to an interest in altered states of consciousness and finally to meditation and Eastern religions. And so it was that I read my first serious books on Buddhism. I found them fascinating and the more I read, the more I was attracted.

Buddhism's doctrines appealed to my logical faculties, while the personality of the Buddha and what he represented appealed to me emotionally. But study, marriage and my work kept me preoccupied. "Some day," I said to myself, "I will study Buddhism in depth." It took almost thirty years for that "some day" to arrive.

A few years ago, having long settled permanently in Singapore, my wife began to practise yoga, which reminded me of my promise made long ago to study Buddhism.

Together we began to attend talks on Eastern religion in general and Buddhism in particular. At an inter-religious conference, the Buddhist representative, a chief monk from a local temple, made a statement that had a profound effect upon me. He said: "Buddhism does not contest or oppose any other religion and it is possible for a Muslim, a Christian, a Jew or a Hindu to practise their faith and simultaneously believe and practise Buddhism." I realised that Buddhism is a way of living and being, rather than a dogma or a faith, and that it does not clash with the beliefs of those who do have dogmas and faiths. Buddhism does not put one in an all or nothing situation; it does not claim to be the final revelation. Rather, it teaches one to understand one's situation and oneself in the constant flow of change. I realised that I was a Buddhist in my thinking but I did not worship or pray to Buddha, like some traditional Buddhists do.

What is it that appeals to me most about Buddhism? It is the emphasis that the Buddha places on the mind, and the potential that is unleashed once the mind is understood and controlled. That our subconscious mind is a treasure house of information is supported by the fact that many important scientific discoveries have been made by intuitive knowledge. Newton's realisation that the earth's gravity keeps the moon in its orbit, Darwin's idea that the species evolved by natural selection and Kekules' discovery of benzene rings are just some of many. I believe that meditation can open up the great powers of the subconscious mind and turn us into new and better human beings.

The Buddha's stress on self-reliance is also very appealing. Shortly before he died, the Buddha was asked who should be looked to as the teacher after he had gone. He replied: "Be an island unto yourselves. Be a refuge unto yourselves. Betake yourselves to no external refuge. Hold fast to the Dhamma as your island and refuge. And those who either now or after I am gone live thus, they will become the highest, but they must be anxious to learn." To me the key sentence here is the last one. Everyone who wishes to understand themselves, their fellows and their world must take the initiative and be anxious to learn.

There are many other aspects of Buddhism that appeal to me. The emphasis on compassion and love which encompasses not only humans but all forms of life, the Noble Eightfold Path which puts virtue and truthfulness beyond all other qualities, the masterly analysis of suffering which pinpoints craving as the main culprit, and the rejection of a fixed personality the misunderstanding of which is responsible for our egoism and selfishness. In short, I find the Buddha's wisdom like a bright light on an otherwise dark and confusing road. I know I cannot run because the path is a gradual one, but I am content to walk on. I am content to watch in awe the mysteries of life, and continue to seek the goal.

Dhammacharini Padmasuri was born in England in 1951. She trained as a nurse, with special training as a midwife. She received her Dhammacharini ordination in 1980 and since 1982 has worked as a nurse and teacher of Buddhism in India.

A Nurse's Story

Dhammacharini Padmasuri

I was born the daughter of an Anglican clergyman in England in 1951. My middle class, secure and fairly happy upbringing was quite strongly Christian. I was expected, though never forced, to go to Church on Sundays, say my prayers before going to bed, and there was a general ambience of caring and respect for others. I found from quite at early age that Christianity gave me an experience of another dimension of life, even a 'spiritual' dimension, though as a teenager the concept of a personal God was beginning to wear a little thin: why didn't a benevolent god prevent drought and famine, wars, earthquakes and disease? These were the kinds of questions I used to ask myself but never found a satisfactory answer for, just a lot of rationalisations. Wanting to 'believe', and unable to call myself an 'atheist' (which seemed almost life denying) I went along with the contradictions.

At the age of 20, having finished school and done a number of quite interesting but not very satisfying jobs, I took up a three-year nursing course with the intention of using that skill in the Third World, something which had attracted me since a young age. On completion, I travelled as a tourist overland from England to India. In retrospect, I was even at that time searching for something, and the East seemed to hold a mystical pull over me. But whatever it was, I was looking for, I didn't find it, at least not in the East. However, I did meet fellow travellers who meditated, and this intrigued me, so on returning to England, I found myself a meditation teacher, as much from curiosity as anything else. This teacher was a member of the 'Western Buddhist Order' who taught meditation practices of mindfulness of breathing (*annapana sati*) and loving-kindness meditation (*metta bhavana*). After a few classes he started introducing aspects of Buddhism, in particular the Noble Eightfold Path. Without having read or even heard much about Buddhism before, I suddenly felt as though his words were being directed entirely at me, and gave an uncanny feeling of 'coming home'. I think I could honestly say that from that moment I hardly looked back.

My involvement and practice of Buddhism went from strength to strength, and I was soon living in a women's Buddhist community, meditating daily, attending classes and courses on Buddhism run by the 'Friends of the Western Buddhist Order' (FWBO), going on retreats, and helping to run a Right Livelihood co-operative business along with other Buddhist women (the profits of which helped support the public Dhamma centre).

Perhaps the most important thing that struck me when I encountered Buddhism was the idea of change, that one could change, and that the Dhamma gave one a practical way in which to bring about that change, especially the practice of meditation. From my own experience I was able to test this out for myself. I found devotional practices particularly helpful in encouraging emotional involvement in the Dhamma, and the practice of *sila* just seemed sensible. The more the Dhamma opened up to me, the more I was convinced that Buddhism was the only path I could follow.

In 1980 I was ordained as Dhammacharini by my teacher, the founder of the 'Western Buddhist Order', Maha Sthavira Sangharakshita, and was given the name Padmasuri (which means 'Lotus heroine', combining the more traditionally feminine qualities of the lotus or 'Padma', with the more traditionally masculine, pioneering, adventurous qualities of 'Suri'). In the three years of my involvement until that point I still had it at the back of my mind that I would like to use my nursing skills in the Third World, but I didn't want to be isolated from the Sangha which was becoming more and more important, I realised, to my growth and development as a Buddhist. Though I had gone for Refuge on my own, as an individual, saying that I would take that step even if nobody else in the world were to do so, there was in fact a Sangha of other men and women who had committed themselves to the same ideals, to the Three Jewels. Spiritual friendship amongst members of the Sangha is, in the Buddha's words, 'the whole of the spiritual life', the FWBO puts much emphasis onto the development of spiritual friendship, and my experience told me that I needed that friendship.

Then in 1982 came the possibility of combining my nursing skills with Buddhism. I was able to help set up a medical project in slum areas in India amongst thousands of the ex-Untouchables who converted to Buddhism in 1956 under the leadership of Dr Bhimrao Ambedkar. Already a few members of the WBO from the West were helping this new Buddhist movement to carry on work that Sangharakshita had started at the time of the conversions. To explain more clearly about this Buddhist Revival in India I will give some historical details.

The Hindu caste system is a system of hereditary and graded inequality, backed by the authority of the Hindu scriptures. Right at the bottom are those who were considered so inherently inferior as to pollute others, and were both called and treated as untouchables. They were denied the dignity and freedom necessary to lead a truly human life. Forced to live outside villages in the most unhealthy quarters, they were allowed to do only the most menial and degrading of work, often having to beg in order to survive. They were not allowed to own property or wear new clothes, and were denied any form of secular or religious education. Though in 1950 the practice of untouchability was declared illegal by the constitution of independent India, bonds forged over centuries take more than laws to break them.

Dr Ambedkar was a great leader of the Untouchable people. He himself suffered immensely from the disadvantages of untouchability throughout his childhood. However, by the 1920's, through extraordinary persistence and courage, he succeeded if becoming the first Untouchable to matriculate, and then helped by two socially-minded Indian rulers, he completed his education in the UK and USA. Eventually he became First Law Minister for free India, and played a leading role in drafting the Indian constitution.

Ambedkar began his work for the Untouchables by trying to reform the caste system from within; however, by 1935 he reached the conclusion that the only way to eradicate untouchability was to make a complete separation from the caste system which was the cause of it. Not wishing to leave his followers with no religion, since he saw the need for spiritual guidance and inspiration, he considered at length to which religion he should turn. Eventually he chose Buddhism, as being the only religion that was both indigenous to India, and which constantly encouraged the highest values in man and the transformation of society, through entirely non-violent means. At an historic ceremony in Nagpur in the centre of India on 14th October 1956, he and some 500,000 followers took the Three Refuges and Five Precepts. Dr Ambedkar knew that if the conversion was to be a success it had to be followed up by proper teaching. Above all, he emphasised that Buddhism was a religion to be practised. Tragically, only six weeks later he died, leaving this new Buddhist movement both leaderless and in a state of shock.

It is this situation in which the FWBO (or Trailokya Bauddha Maha Sangha (TBMSG), as this movement is called in Indian) is working. At the time of the conversions, Maha Sthavira Sangharakshita was living in India, and was both a trusted friend and adviser to Ambedkar. Sangharakshita spent the winter months of every year after the untimely death of Ambedkar, working and teaching in the villages and towns amongst the new converts to Buddhism. In 1964, after 20 years as a Buddhist monk in India, he returned to his native England and founded the Western Buddhist Order.

In 1978 he encouraged an English disciple, Dhammachari Lokamitra, to resume the work he had started there so many years before. As a result, TBMSG was set up in 1979, and before long there was a resurgence of Dhamma activity in Maharashtra in western India.

So, it was into this very different world that I stepped in 1982: children dying of malnutrition, women looking haggard in their early twenties after numerous pregnancies, men turning to illicit liquor, families often of ten or more living in stifling tin huts on urban wasteland, hundreds of similar huts bunched together in shanty-towns criss-crossed by open gutters, toil, sweat, poverty and disease...

For three years, my main involvement in India was with medical work in the slums, particularly with mothers and children and with an emphasis on preventive medicine. I was working alongside an English doctor, also a member of the WBO. Through this work, I began to understand something of the Indian people and their culture. I made friends, and despite the dire living conditions of others, often experienced a warmth and positivity that left me astounded. Although the medical work continues to both thrive and expand, it is now run totally by Indians, and I am no longer working as a nurse. Instead, I spend my time teaching Buddhism, mostly to ex-Untouchable women who live in the city slums. I take classes and study groups, teach meditation, organise and lead retreats, and I am invited to give talks in cities and villages all over the state of Maharashtra.

The Buddha's teachings are a path to freedom. In reply to Mahaprajapati Gotami's searching question, "What is your Dhamma?" the Buddha stated that it is whatever helps man to evolve -"whatever in practice conduces to peace of mind, purity, seclusion, stillness of desire, detachment of the world, the transcendental..." But how does this work out in practice and in detail?

Buddhist practice rests on the foundation of ethical behaviour. All Buddhists undertake to observe five precepts,
or 'training principles', thus trying to cultivate loving
kindness, generosity, sexual contentment, truthful com-
munication and clarity of mind. In the cramped, oppressive
conditions of city slums, where atrocities such as wife
beating, communal violence and child labour are common,
these simple precepts have a dramatic effect. The 'evil' of
liquor is a common cause of some of the worst excesses,
hence the fifth precept - of abstention from all intoxicants
that cloud the mind - is taken very literally by Indian
Buddhists.

Buddhism is in accord with reason. It has nothing to do
with the kind of blind beliefs that prevent one from
taking responsibility for one's own and other's welfare.
I have known children to die unnecessarily from measles
because outside intervention during illness was considered
'bad luck'.

Encountering the superstition and devaluation of man
within the caste-ridded Hindu society, I came to see
more and more how Buddhism, by contrast, encourages
the highest values both in man and society, and offers
practical methods for their development. Meditation, for
example, is a tool for the systematic cultivation of clearer,
happier states of mind. Through meditation, people gain
a vision and perspective, a more creative way of 'being',
both in themselves and in relation to others, that their
cramped and hectic lives won't normally allow. Of course,
meditation alone won't improve the society in which one
lives, so in India as in the West, Buddhists are encouraged
to work together on Right Livelihood projects, empha-

sising co-operation on the basis of common ideals.

Living and working with Buddhists in India, I came to
see more and more how Buddhism is a universal religion,
which has no place for notions of social inequality. It
can be practised by men and women, young and old, by
people of any race, class or colour. Whether one is living
in a Bombay slum or a luxury Manhattan apartment,
one can, if one chooses, practise the Dhamma.

The Dhamma is a means of self-development, and the
more an individual grows, the more of an impact he or
she will have on society. It is not that social work is not
needed; you don't teach a starving man to meditate, first
you give him food. But solely tackling socio-economic
problems in terms of providing resources, passing on
skills, giving education and so on, doesn't go far enough.
It is by no means necessarily the case that material
suffering has exclusively material causes. I know several
Indian families who have managed to get education and
jobs, who have moved out of the slums, turning their
backs on their less fortunate brothers and sisters, prefer-
ring the material and social benefits of their new-found
status, yet who continue to suffer through their greed,
hatred and ignorance. Conversely, I know of people who
have never had such opportunities, but who through
their practice of the Dhamma have made far more dramatic changes within themselves.

India is a strongly patriarchal society, and women have
little opportunity of really expressing themselves. From
the early days that TBMSG established itself in India,
retreats and classes were for men and women combined,

but it was found that very few women participated in these activities, and when they did, they remained quiet and passive. Since I have been able to hold women-only events, the number of women coming along has increased quite dramatically. I often hold one to four day retreats now, attended by over 100 women, and they are far from passive.

Traditionally, a woman's role in Indian society is one of serving, particularly serving men: her father, her brothers, her husband, her sons. So when she comes away into the countryside on retreat, with other women only, it is perhaps the first time she has left her home alone in her whole life. She may at first feel a little strange, insecure, even bewildered. But her faith in Dr Ambedkar has brought her to find out for herself exactly what the Dhamma is about and how she can become a truly practising Buddhist. After only two or three days one can see remarkable changes.

After retreats, many return to their villages of city slums and take up a daily meditation practice, and if literate, start reading various TBMSG Dhamma publications. They may go to weekly classes where again meditation is taught along with the practical study of the Dhamma, and new friendships with like-minded people will start to develop. Some of these women have been seriously studying and practising the Dhamma for a number of years now, so that by 1987, two Indian women were ready to take the step of ordination. The Dhammacharini Ordination within TBMSG represents the public acknowledgment of one's commitment to put both the ideals and the practice of Buddhism at the very centre of one's life, and to arrange every other aspect of one's life accordingly. In other words, commitment to the Three Jewels and the taking of ten precepts is primary, and to a large degree reflects one's commitment. So the two Indian Dhammacharinis are both mothers and wives, but are without doubt sincerely committed to their own and others' development.

I haven't always found it easy living in India; the social conditioning, particularly of the women, is so very different from my own, and yet I soon came to realise that what we have in common is so much more important than the externals. Doing the medical work first gave me a good knowledge of Indian women and the particular problems they face, so that when I came to do more Dhamma teaching, I was able to adapt the teachings to make them relevant, hopefully without distorting the essence. It has made me think a lot more. In England it was easy to repeat various teachings rather glibly, without necessarily understanding much, using familiar words, even cliches without much thought as to their real meaning but in India, many of the women I teach are illiterate, so for them, conceptual formulations are often not appropriate. Practical examples and similes are better understood, which in turn means that I have to be very clear myself on the real meaning of a teaching to be able to convey it clearly to others.

The heat, dirt and noise of India are not always easy conditions in which to work, and yet the response of people to the Dhamma is so whole-hearted, that the compensation for working here is far greater than any difficulties. In fact, because of the conditions, I have found myself being more whole-hearted, and there is less to distract me than in England in terms of 'pleasurable' alternatives, although of course the mind is always fickle!

In the six years I've been in India I feel my own commitment, my own 'going for refuge' has both deepened and broadened, and I think I've learned to be more adaptable, also more sincere. I am not sure how much longer I shall be working in India, but I feel quite privileged to have had the opportunity to help re-establish the Dhamma in the very land of its birth, being part of 'The Dhamma Revolution'.

Venerable Dhammika was born in Australia in 1951 and developed an interest in Buddhism in his teens. He received his lower ordination in India and moved to Sri Lanka where he taught meditation for several years in the Kandy district. In 1985 he received his higher ordination in Singapore, where he teaches at the Education Department's Curriculum Development Institute, and where he also acts as spiritual advisor to several Buddhist organisations.

My Quest for Happiness

Ven. S. Dhammika

I was born the second child of ordinary middle-class Australian parents, both of whom come from English stock. Although they were married in church and called themselves Christians, my parents' attitude to religion might have been described as 'Church of England indifference'.

For as far back as I can remember, I was fascinated by mythology and religion. Even when quite young, I would leaf through encyclopaedias and art books and stare in wonder at Egyptian gods with their strange, half-human half-animal bodies, and the gods of ancient Greece and Rome.

The Greek gods and heroes interested me most, and when I was old enough to read I acquainted myself with the legends and stories about them. I prided myself on being able to pronounce their names and recite their individual biographies, and I think I felt, in some strange way, that these gods were not phantoms of the imagination but that they were real. Whether this was a child's imagination or the first expression of the urge to know what the Buddha called amata, the Immortal, I cannot say.

My first formal instruction in Christianity came in primary school when one lesson a week was reserved for Religious Instruction. I loved to listen to Old Testament stories like Noah's Ark and the Egyptian captivity, and the parables of Jesus from the New Testament. Certainly the teacher, a lay volunteer, noticed my attention, and after class one day she took me aside and asked me if I would like to start going to church. I would meet new friends, she said, and learn to serve and love God. So with my mother's consent, I would set out to church each Sunday morning with two shillings in one pocket for the collection and a shilling in the other pocket to spend on the way home, although it did not always work out that way. It was not long before God's presence became apparent. If I scratched my back while climbing through a barbed wired fence, I would try to recall some commandment I had broken and I could always find something. God, I said to myself, was punishing me for my sins. If I did something wrong and just managed to escape getting caught, God, I said, was giving me a second chance. It was clear to me that I was being constantly watched, warned, rewarded and punished. This naive conception of God is not just the creation of a child's mind, as I now discover when I meet and talk to Christians of fundamentalist persuasion.

Soon after I entered high school, I got to know a class-mate who, like me, took religion seriously and attended church regularly. It was encouraging to meet someone with similar interests, but when I told him what I believed and which church I went to, he shook his head dismissingly saying, "That's not what Jesus taught and that's not the true church." The boldness and confidence with which he said this and the Bible quotes he used to back up his claims (he always carried a well-thumbed Bible), left me confused and uncertain and within a very short time I had changed my views and my church.

The Presbyterian church that I now began to attend was completely different from what I was used to. Although I enjoyed my time at the Church of England, for the most part, the congregation were not my own age, the hymns were solemn and the atmosphere was generally uninspiring. Now I was in the company of people my own age who were friendly, enthusiastic and, or so it seemed to me, very happy being Christians. There were singing and get-togethers, and the Bible was studied in minute detail. Great emphasis was given to getting our beliefs right, and the slightest misunderstanding or divergence from what was considered the truth was quickly corrected by referring to the Bible. I joined the Boys' Brigade, a sort of Presbyterian Boy Scouts, and was generally kept pretty busy. But being kept occupied on the one hand, and being constantly told that Christians are happy, on the other, could not disguise the fact that I was not happy. In fact, difficulties in my parents' marriage and poor marks at school, compounded with the usual problems of adolescence, were all making me very unhappy. Praying to God certainly made me feel better, but it did not really change things.

One Sunday, we were being taught the Old Testament story about Abraham and his son, and as the story unfolded the teacher was illustrating each event by placing cut-out paper figures on a felt-covered board. First the altar, then Abraham with the sacrificial knife raised, and finally the angel stopping the sacrifice at the last moment. The point of the story, the teacher said, was that we must obey God's commandments completely, for even if they appear wrong to us, God undoubtedly had a plan that we could not understand. The vividness with which this story was told and the moral behind it shocked me. So deep was my shock, in fact, that I completely forgot myself and began to debate with the teacher. "Surely it could not be right to prepare to kill your own son just because God said so!" I said. "Abraham should have checked and checked again." The teacher countered that with our limited wisdom we could not possibly fathom God's will. "What would you do," I said, "if a revelation told you to sacrifice your son?" I could see from the expression on the teacher's face that he had never considered this possibility before and when he collected himself, he restated his case in less emphatic terms, trying to undo the damage he had inadvertently done. But it was too late; faith, like sand slipping through the fingers, fell away from me and I began to reassess everything I had previously taken for granted. About six months after the events I have just described, I sat with my head down and my eyes closed while the pastor lead the prayer. He addressed God in the first person as if he were actually in the church. I opened my eyes and looked at the faces of the others in the congregation. Some displayed expressions of devotion, some of repentance, some of supplication. They all seemed to feel something, some thing they would probably call God's presence or at least a response to his presence. Then I turned my attention to myself and found that I felt nothing. I closed my eyes and tried to absorb myself in the prayer and to feel devotion, but I felt absolutely nothing. I reviewed my motivation for attending church and the Boys' Brigade, and with a suddenness that made me sit up and open my eyes, I saw that I was going for the fellowship, the sense of belonging and the atmosphere created by the hymns and music. When I did feel something, it was induced by all these things and I was being told that it was the presence of God. I saw now very clearly that it was not. After the service I walked out of the church and never went back again.

One day I happened to pick up a book on Tibet, and although it was a travel story, it did make quite a few references to Buddhism. The author mentioned that although Tibetans lived hard lives in a harsh environment, they were the most cheerful people he had ever met, something he attributed to Buddhism. He said that because Buddhism teaches respect for all life, wild birds and animals showed a remarkable lack of fear toward humans. This, plus the author's adventures in Tibet, enthralled me, and the next time I went to the library I looked for a book on Buddhism. There was exactly one, *The Mind Unshaken*, by the British journalist John Walters. I took it home, and as I read it, I had the feeling, not that I was learning some thing new, but rather that I was remembering something that I had once known but forgotten. Like the last pieces of a jig-saw puzzle, each idea I read about fell quickly into place and I soon had a complete picture. When I finished the book, after spending the better part of the night reading it, I knew I was a Buddhist. The ideas that all forms of life, even animals, are worthy of our compassion, that each person has the potential for enlightenment, and that the origin and working of the universe could be understood in terms of natural causation, all made perfect sense to me. Some teachings, like rebirth for example, were less easy to accept, but it was reassuring to learn that, rather than force myself to blindly believe, I was asked to suspend judgement for the time being and get along with applying what I could understand. I started to call myself a Buddhist and over the next couple of years, I read everything I could on this wonderful teaching.

Although I was confident that I was now facing in the right direction, I could not help feeling that my journey towards Nirvana had still not really begun. I had exchanged Christian dogmas for Buddhist concepts, which while being more intellectually satisfying, were still just concepts. I had never practised meditation and I knew nothing of the exalted states of consciousness or profound spiritual experiences which the Buddha referred to so often. And so in the early 1970's, like thousands of other young Westerners, I set out for the East, not with the intention of sightseeing, but to visit the Buddhist holy places and, I hoped, to become a monk.

India exposed its diversity to me unashamedly and with the suddenness of a slap in the face. Everything was strange, interesting, even shocking, but when I was at Buddhist shrines or holy places, I was comfortable and happy. At Bodh Gaya, as I sat in a tea shop, listening to two Americans discussing meditation, I saw immaculate Japanese pilgrims alighting from air-conditioned buses, scruffy Tibetans doing their prostrations and a party of saffron robed Laotian monks chanting together under the Bodhi tree. This, together with the strange booming music from the Tibetan temple that woke me in the morning and the beautiful Pali chanting that I sat and listened to in the great Maha Bodhi Temple each evening, made me realise the richness of the Buddhist tradition, how timeless its message was, how universal its appeal. This was not dead concepts; this was living practice.

The next place I went to on my pilgrimage, Shravasti, had been a great city at the time of the Buddha but now, as if to testify to the truth of impermanence, it was a mass of ruins covered with dry jungle and inhabited by jackals. An old monk, Venerable Sangharatana, lived in a temple on the site and looked after the few pilgrims who came that way. I had planned to stay two days, but Venerable Sangharatana's friendliness and knowing that the Buddha had lived here longer than anywhere else caused me to stay for months. Venerable Sangharatana had an unshakable faith in the Dhamma; he was good-humoured and so unaffected and without guile, that his occasional volatile tone and his childlike weakness for sweets only seemed to emphasise his easy naturalness. Since that time, I have met Buddhist monks who were far more spiritually developed than Venerable Sangharatana, but rarely have I met any so approachable and ready to laugh. He was perfectly imperfect.

I took my novice ordination at Shravasti and later went to Sri Lanka to pursue further studies. There I stayed in a monastery where the monks, constantly delighted that someone would come so far to learn what they knew, generously shared their knowledge of Pali, monastic discipline and Buddhist scriptures with me. Eventually I moved to the cool mountain town of Kandy and established a small hermitage where I could live, study and meditate in solitude. A few years ago, just before I left Sri Lanka, my youngest brother came from Australia to visit me. When he saw where and how I lived in a two-room hut without power or running water, sleeping on the floor and begging for my food, he asked with incredulity, "Are you happy?" I stopped for a moment and thought about what the Buddha's teachings had given me, how they had changed me and what they promised one who practices them. I thought of the several teachers I had met whose lives seemed to be living proof that spiritual transformation is possible and how their example had given me the strength and patience to deal with my own defilements. And I answered, "Yes I am happy, very happy indeed."

Chester Dee was born in 1959 in the Philippines and attended De LaSalle University where he graduated summa cum laude *in Mathematics. He worked as a corporate planner before earning a Masters degree in Business Administration at the University of Chicago. Since then, he has worked with a number of major international banks in Singapore and London.*

A Search Fulfilled

Chester Dee

How does one lose faith in a religion and convert to another? For some, a new faith comes as a sudden experience of the extraordinary, an experience that is attributed to a supernatural influence. For others, it comes as a chance meeting with a teacher after years of seeking and wandering and sampling from here and there like a gourmet in search of some new diet. For some, it comes only after much independent thought and comparison, while for others, it comes with a casual invitation of a friend to a religious meeting.

But for me, the Dharma came quite slowly - in drops that barely formed trickles. The way was quite uneventful, and therefore there were no vivid experiences that could act as a sharp dividing line between one phase of conversion and the next. I did see old age, sickness and death - but unlike the Buddha, I did not understand.

The earliest thing I remember that consumed my attention, in the relatively strict Chinese Catholic household that I grew up in, was the phenomenon of light. Nothing seemed so vivid and yet so intangible, so ubiquitous and yet so mysterious, as the glow of a bulb, the radiance of the sun, the soft twinkling of the stars. So from an early age I took to lamps, lighthouses, fire, crystals, and prisms when most of my playmates were interested in bicycles, guns, bows and arrows. This interest in light was to shape the years of my life from childhood to adolescence and even beyond. For one thing, it initiated a deep preoccupation with physics, and later, with mathematics.

There was, however, another sort of light that concerned me. This was the warm inner glow that welled up in me whenever I heard the soft, undulating cadence of the Gregorian chant as it rose, inextricably entwined with the resinous vapours of incense that poured out of the bishop's censer as he swung it before the monstrance - a sublime aspiration to Him Who was the Source of all existence, the Creator of all things visible and invisible. And from some dark portion of my mind came a faint hunch that perhaps this interior light and the one outside were somehow connected. Perhaps they were one light, split ages ago and now seeking to re-unite. That was history - a long slow evolution wherein little bits of illumination (that collectively formed this world) were somehow struggling to come together, to rejoice in some higher unity where alone final rest could be found.

With these sorts of thoughts whirling in my mind it was no wonder that I turned to Vedanta. Whether we were dewdrops that sought to merge with the shining sea, or there was only the shining sea whose waves had not realised their identity - it did not matter. What was important was the shining sea -Brahman, one without a second. Spiritual practice revolved around stilling every movement of body, breath, and mind until absolute being, consciousness, and bliss could shine through.

During this period there was very little I could read on Buddhism - what could one expect from a primary school library? There were, however, some intuitive learnings in that direction. I remember my parents bringing me to Taiwan where I heard about the giant Buddha image in the middle of the island. For several days I kept on insisting, of course without really knowing why, on seeing the image. My parents finally relented, and together we took the four-hour train trip. Thereafter, whenever we went to Taiwan I made it a point to visit as many temples as possible, carefully distinguishing the Buddhist ones from the Taoist shrines.

But for the most part, my study of Vedanta continued until the middle of high school, where I had a much larger library open to me. There I came across a book by the celebrated psychologist Carl Jung. The passage that caught my attention dealt with individuation - the psychological process by which a human being became a whole. As Jung conceived it, this occurred when a new centre of experience evolved between one's personal consciousness and the collective unconscious (a timeless portion of the mind which all humans have in common, and where various primordial archetypal forces have their roots). A new centre! I kind of expected that at the supreme moment one's own consciousness would dissolve tracelessly back into the collective unconscious. But a new centre of being in which two separate parts of the mind were brought to mutual fulfilment instead of being meaninglessly regressed back to some primitive unity - this novel dimension was to dramatically shift the axis of my viewpoint. To seek to withdraw into some absolute struck me as a spiritual death in which uniformity was mistaken for unity, numbness for peace, abstraction for reality. I began to see how, as the Buddha had observed, the craving for absolute being was the craving for annihilation in another guise. The spiritual quest lay not in a blank suppression of all thoughts and movements, but in the purification and unfoldment of the deepest forces and the highest aspirations in our psyche until they were brought together in a unity that was not stagnant but vital and dynamic. In order to accomplish all this, what was required was not to submerge oneself in some kind of blind absorption, but to develop a clarity and comprehension that could penetrate and transform one's mind from its very roots.

This experience of integration, I realised, was embodied in the Mahayana Buddhist explanation of the Three Bodies (*Trikaya*) of the Buddha. However, it was only much later that I came to understand how intimately it was connected with the fundamental insight of dependent origination which, as the Buddha tells Kaccana in the *Samyutta Nikaya*, is free from the extremes of being and non-being. Vedanta is based on the idea of absolute being - Brahman is one without a second - and implicitly on non-being as well, since the plurality of appearance is denied. But, as Buddhism had often pointed out, being and non-being are merely artificial reifications of dynamic inter-relationships. By replacing these concepts with the view of interdependent origination (and its corollary, *sunyata*) Mahayana Buddhism was able firstly, to replace the Hindu ideal of static absorption into Brahman with the more dynamic ideal of the bodhisattva's Non-abiding Nirvana; and secondly, to replace the Vedanta affirmation of unity/denial of the plurality with the Dhammadhatu Totality of perfect Buddhahood, in which the universal and the individual mutually interpenetrated without obstruction. It therefore seemed to me that the Mahayana path was one that involved fully developing

the qualities (*paramitas*) of one's innate Buddha-poten-
tial so that they purified, perfected, and balanced each
other in a higher synthesis - as opposed to a path in
which everything was seen to be identically one without
any true differentiation whatsoever, or to a path which
involved the withdrawal of the Knower (**Purusha**) from
Nature (**Prakriti**). The Hindu teaching of absorption into
Brahman on the one hand, and the Buddhist teaching of
interdependent origination and integration on the other,
implied different spiritual paths and fruitions.

However, while whatever slight knowledge of Buddhism
I possessed had made me cease to look at Hinduism as a
path for me, at this point, it still did not occur to me to
become a Buddhist. For one thing, there was not enough
material available to me at that time with which to
develop my understanding. In contrast, my environment
was correctly set up for Roman Catholicism - the people
were Catholic, and abundant material on Christian theology
and scholasticism was available both in the library and
in the local bookstores. In light of what I said above, it
should be no surprise that the Christian doctrine of the
hypostatic union - in which Christ was declared to be
simultaneously true God and true man - had especially
great appeal to me. The reforms of Vatican II and the
extensive use of existential phenomenology transformed
the standard catechism into a positive way of living,
through which alienated man could find his way back to
God. I was exultantly swept into the triumphant redis-
covery of the Christian faith.

Catholic life for me drew its sustenance from three spiritual
activities: contemplation, liturgy, and work. The practice of contemplation has three stages. First, one takes a

specific verse of scripture, an incident in the life of Christ, or perhaps a particular aspect of the faith as one's starting point and receives it into one's heart as if it were directly coming from Christ Himself. My favourite topics were the central mysteries around which Christianity hinges: the Holy Trinity (which declares that even in the most sublime unity of the Godhead there is the plurality of persons), the Incarnation (in which God and man are united in Christ), the Redemption ("Dying He destroyed our death, Rising He restored our life"), and the mystical body of Christ of which we are the parts (Christ the head, and the Holy Spirit the soul). Second, one lets the chosen theme unfold in one's heart and mind, so that one could discover the divine inspiration and grace enshrined in the subject and allow it to permeate one's life, like deep calling unto deep. Finally, having received God's message and invitation, one responds to the Divine Presence by raising one's soul and will in prayer, remembering that God's delight in benefiting man is greater than man's delight in receiving the benefit.

Liturgy meant the celebration of the gift of the Divine Life and the actual effectuation of sanctifying grace through the seven sacraments. The central role here was occupied by the Holy Sacrifice of the Mass in which the mystery of Christ's redemption was renewed in the souls of those who participated.

Whatever blessings and graces one received through contemplation and liturgy were to be allowed to transform one's daily life. Work was to be a perpetual offering and prayer to the Almighty, and hence a primary means of sanctification.

I pursued this Catholic way of life for a number of years. However, my involvement with Christianity did not put an end to my study of other religions. I was still deeply interested in comparative religion, and thought that some day my studies in that area would prove useful in introducing Christianity to those of other persuasions (especially Buddhists, ironically). Nevertheless, I was always very careful to maintain in my research the distinction between natural philosophy and Christian revelation, which alone was the final guide to Heaven.

It was only much later, in my senior years in the university, that Buddhism once more made an impact on my life. On the one hand I had more money to buy books, and on the other I discovered new specialised bookshops for those interested in Oriental religion. These factors, together with the maturity of outlook university life was developing in me, rekindled my avid interest in Buddhism. For the first time in my life, I had an adequate number of sutra translations, commentaries, and interpretations. My reading made a deep impact on me.

I was impressed by the whole range of attainments proclaimed possible by the Buddha. Through the path of virtue (in both its negative sense of avoiding the unwholesome and its positive sense of cultivating the wholesome), a bountiful human birth or a blissful heavenly realm could be obtained; through the path of *samadhi*, the eight *jhanas* with their assorted heavens in the realm of form as well as in the formless realm; through the path of insight, the supramundane states of the Arhat, or the Pratekyabuddha, or the Samyaksambuddha. This is not to mention the methods outlined by the Buddha for the attainment of

the six classes of psychic power and the various transcendental states outlined in the Abhidharma tradition,
nor for that matter the various attainments given in the
Mahayana and Vajrayana traditions. Faced with this
veritable encyclopaedia of spirituality, I could not help
but doubt the comprehensiveness of Christianity.

I was impressed by the various spiritual faculties, powers, knowledges, and *samadhis* attributed to the Realised
Ones, which made me doubt faith and love as primary
organs of religious experience, especially when unsupported by wisdom. My ideas of faith at that time were
still of the romantic sort, extolling faith as being darkness to reason but illumination for the heart. I cried with
the early Church Fathers: "I believe that Christ died for
me because it is incredible; I believe He rose from the
dead because it is impossible". But now I wondered why
I might as well not believe in everything incredible and
impossible.

I was impressed by the uncanny way in which Buddhism
could single out the truly basic issues of spirituality, as
when the Buddha stripped naked the nature of man's
craving for existence instead of covering it up by the
promise of an eternal heaven; and by the way the Dharma
revealed a higher perspective in which those things which
were once thought to be basic issues were seen to be
secondary (and in fact the result of fundamental errors
in evaluating experience), as in the issue of being and
non-being. The formal doctrinal system of Buddhism
was no doubt awesome, but what struck me more was
the way the Buddha asked the right sort of questions.
Obtaining true insight into the causes and nature of our

religious aspirations was at least as important as the religious system adopted to fulfil those aspirations, otherwise God and Brahman became mere havens for the security of the ego. I realised that Christian doctrine tacitly made assumptions about self and God and then wove a theological tapestry from there, whereas it seemed that spirituality lay more in examining these deep-rooted assumptions to see how they affected our views on religion and the quality of our religious experience.

The unexpected brilliance of this so-called pagan religion, and the "come and see" fearlessness with which it was proclaimed, caused me to search almost frantically for ways and means by which Christianity could define itself as unique and final. I began with the traditional distinction between the natural order, discernible by reason, and a supernatural order and life that would have been completely unknown had it not been revealed by God to man through the prophets and the apostles, and which had been enshrined and summed up in the Holy Bible. But how do we know that this is God's revelation? Because the prophets had said God had spoken to them? But there were countless prophets - both ancient and modern, who had claimed this. If one simply accepts their word through faith, then why not believe in the Hindu rishis, or the Mongolian shamans? And closer to home, why not accept the Gospel of St. Peter, or the ancient scriptures of the Christian Gnostics?

There had to be something in the content of scripture itself that was outstanding, unique, and final - that could stamp it once and for all as revelation. But when I examined the scriptures, being careful not to read in my preconceived theological notions, there was nothing in it like this at all. There was a collection of myths, laws, and folk wisdom; there were histories, biographies, and comforting words - but nothing of importance that could not be found in older material. In fact, there was much that was expressed more clearly and more movingly in the literature of other religious traditions.

Or perhaps the Church was right in declaring the theological mysteries of faith to be the central revelation - the Trinity, the Incarnation, and so on. But then if this were so, why couldn't the Bible state these all-important tenets clearly and categorically? In many cases, these articles of faith could be derived only by interpretations that struck me as rather convoluted - one might as well derive them from the *Iliad* or the *Odyssey*, as in fact the ancient Greeks had done.

I had personally held that the chief theme of the Bible's revelation was the personhood of Christ. In Christ, God showed His love by becoming man in order to bridge the chasm of sin that separated us from His divine life. But then why not believe in the Hindu avatars such as Krishna?

All in all, the Bible seemed to be a document from which generation upon generation of Church fathers, scholars, preachers and evangelists tried to extract spiritual meaning. No doubt they succeeded, but perhaps the job would have been much easier if they used the *Bhagavad Gita* or the Confucian *Analects*. Much of the spiritual wisdom attributed to the Bible came more from the interpretations afforded to it than from the text itself. The situation reminded me of the story of the hungry traveller who, in order to induce a stingy woman to let him in, told her that he had a nail that could make soup. While the nail was boiling in the pot of water over a fire, the traveller persuaded the woman to add a bit of this and a bit of that to make the "nail soup" taste better. In the end the soup was indeed rich and delicious, but what was the nail for?

After inquiring into the nature of revelation, I turned to its significance for the spiritual life. Does a belief in the Bible as God's word and an acceptance of Jesus Christ as one's personal Lord and Saviour transform our life for the better? I have no doubt that in many cases they indeed do -but what sort of transformation occurs? What were authentic transformations? How did this differ from the transformation experienced by couples falling in love, or by scientists contemplating the universe, or by rishis in intense *samadhi*? All of them experienced a change that made them happier, wiser, more full of love and tolerance to a degree that in many cases exceeded that of a pious Christian. In fact, in some cases, the motives, thoughts, and actions arising from Christian converts and evangelists were simply manifestations on a different level of the same hatred, clinging, fanaticism, and closed-minded ignorance that pervades the ordinary human mind. Were these saved by Christ? Wasn't the approach to religion outlined in the *Tevijja Sutta* a saner way? Even God as He reveals Himself in the Bible often appears to be angry, jealous, and vengeful. I felt that it was crucial to reveal by insight the causes, nature, significance of the various orders of spiritual experience, and that this was a basic spiritual issue which was not really properly addressed in Christianity.

The Buddha, on the other hand, continually emphasised how all religious experiences were to be thoroughly comprehended by insight. He had often mentioned how various idealogies, dogmas, and beliefs arose through a basic misinterpretation of one's religious ecstasy, and had pointed out what sorts of experiences and faculties were beneficial in what way for the realisation of Enlightenment. In the Buddha's distinction between a mind wherein the defilements were still manifest (or only temporarily suppressed) and a mind wherein they had been completely and permanently destroyed, I found a better criterion for the deliberation of the mundane and the supramundane than in the Christian distinction between reason and revelation (a distinction which rapidly blurs when spirituality rather than dogma is being emphasised).

At this stage I also endeavoured to find Christianity's objections to Buddhism. Most of these, such as the charge of nihilism and pessimism, were the standard sort of accusations that were met by Buddhism with refutations that today have become almost equally standard. However, I read one article by a Catholic prelate which divided the religious traditions of mankind into three classes: the animistic religions, which were expressive of basic instinctual drives; the mentalistic religions, which were psychological therapies; and the spiritual religions, which were the result of an invitation and a response. The distinction made between the psychological and spiritual religions seemed to be that the former were similar to engineering the mind, whereas the latter was the outcome of an assent to God's invitation for a supernatural relationship. The distinction between natural and supernatural I had tackled before, but the distinction between mechanical engineering and spirituality had a ring of truth in it. In certain traditions of Buddhism in particular, we see attempts to explain everything away by reducing all spirituality into a precisely measured click-clack of atomic pluralism, and to depict meditation as an intellectual classification of movements into such artificial categories as "lifting, lifting" or "placing, placing". In so doing, I felt that they had missed the point of the Buddha's analysis of the human being into the five aggregates/ *skhandas* which was to reveal the non-clinging spaciousness and dynamic nature of all life. A presentation of paths and fruits must not be taken to mean that Enlightenment can be manufactured by the mere accumulation of meditations, and insight should not be taken as cold-eyed scrutiny explaining things away so that we lose all sense of wonder, awe, and inspiration. All this is made clear by the sutras themselves, especially the Mahayana sutras, and it is in fact said that the Mahayana itself arose as an objection to the ossification and misinterpretation that came as a result of the scholar's penchant for classification and mechanical precision. The Catholic prelate's article, therefore, made me wary of certain interpretations of the Dharma, and highlighted to me how important it was to take Buddhism as a living tradition in which the different schools acted as "check and balance" so that the spirit of Dharma was preserved and yet not mummified.

In this way, the Buddhist approach drew my attention and so permeated my thinking that it soon became senseless to pretend that I was still a strict Christian in outlook. But to actually enter the Dharma, mere intellectual assent was not enough. The decisive point was to be truly inspired by the Buddha's example and to take the Dharma as one's practice as best one can - and this was a step that would only come much later for me. And now in writing all this, I look back at all the non-Buddhist traditions I have passed through, filled with gratefulness for having known them. Whatever little understanding of them that I have accumulated has invited in me a deeper appreciation of the Dharma as universal law. Nevertheless, as the river ultimately must find its way to the ocean, my confidence has come to rest in Him, the Exalted One, completely and perfectly enlightened, the Tathagata. He has become to me the utter consummation of all that I have ever held spiritually meaningful in my life.

Thubten Chodron was born in the United States in 1950. She graduated with a B.A. in History from the University of California at Los Angeles in 1971. She worked as a teacher in the Los Angeles City School System while doing postgraduate work in education at U.C.L.A.. Since taking her novice ordination in 1977, she has taught and studied in India, Nepal, France and Italy, Hong Kong and Singapore. She received her higher ordination in Taiwan in 1986.

You're Becoming a What?:
The Story of an American Buddhist Nun

Ven. Thubten Chodron

When people ask me to talk about my life, I usually start with: "Once upon a time...." Why? Because this life is like a dream bubble, a temporary thing - it is here and then gone, happening once upon a time.

I grew up in America, in a suburb of Los Angeles, doing everything ordinary middle-class children do: going to school and on family vacations, playing with my friends and taking music lessons. My teenage years coincided with the Vietnam War and the protests against racial and sexual discrimination that were widespread in America at that time. These events had a profound effect on an inquisitive and thoughtful child, and I began to question: "Why do people fight wars? Why can't people get along with each other? Why do people judge others merely on the shape and color of their bodies, not on what they are inside? Why do people die? Why are people in the richest country on earth unhappy when they have money and possessions? Why do people who love each other later get divorced? If there is God, why did he make us? Why did he create suffering? What is the meaning of life if all we do is die at the end? What can I do to help others? Is there a perfect society?"

Like every child who wants to learn, I started asking other people - teachers, parents, rabbis, priests. My family was Jewish, though not very religious. The community I grew up in was Christian, so I knew the best and worst of both religions. My Sunday school teachers and the rabbi were not able to answer my questions because they could not give a good reason why God created us and what the purpose of our life was. My boyfriend was Catholic, so I asked the priests too. But I could not understand why a compassionate God would punish people, and why, if he were omnipotent, he didn't do something to stop the suffering in the world. My Christian friends said not to question, just have faith and then I would be saved. However, that contradicted my scientific education in which investigation and understanding were emphasized as the way to wisdom.

Both Judaism and Christianity instruct us to "love thy neighbor," which certainly makes sense. But no one said how to, and I didn't see much brotherly love in practice. Rather, Christian history is littered with the corpses of thousands of people who have been killed in the name of Christ. Some of my schoolteachers were open to discussing these issues, but they, too, had no answers. In the end, some people with kind intentions told me: "Just don't think so much. Go out with your friends and enjoy life." Still, it seemed to me that there must be more to life than having fun, working, making money, having a family, growing old and dying. For lack of a sensible and comprehensive philosophy or religion to guide my life, I became a devout atheist.

I went to university, graduating from U.C.L.A. in history in 1971. The university years were full, because in addition to studies, boyfriends, peace demonstrations, and volunteer work in the ghetto, I had to work as a laboratory assistant in research projects in order to support myself. Although

I graduated Phi Beta Kappa, I was disillusioned with an educational system that emphasized rote learning over creativity, career training for making money over thinking how to correct social injustice, poverty and human problems. Still, I appreciate very much all that my parents and teachers did for me, for their kindness was great.

After graduation, I travelled around the U.S. in a big yellow bakery van, going camping in national parks with my friends. That was the hippy era and also a happy time. One important thing I learned during this period was that if I am not happy with myself, I cannot be happy with others.

I have always felt a wish and a responsibility to help others and to make the world a better place. Education is critical in this process. That is why, upon going back to Los Angeles, I got a job in a school. A year later, I married a young lawyer whom I had met at university. Wanting to look beyond our sheltered upbringings and learn more about the human experience, we stored away our wedding presents and went overseas. For a year and a half we travelled in Europe, North Africa, the Middle East and went overland to India and Nepal. We lived simply, and so had much contact with the people in each country we visited. This was quite an eye-opening experience and a time of much internal exploration as well.

Our funds depleted, we returned to the States. My husband got a job working as a lawyer for poor people, while I went to graduate school at the University of Southern California and taught in the Los Angeles City School System. From my heart, I wanted to help the children, but so often I did not know how to, or could not because I was angry at them. My questions were still there, and although I occasionally discussed them with friends, I was also getting more and more into enjoying life and all the sense pleasures it has to offer.

During summer vacation in 1975, I saw a poster at a bookstore about a meditation course to be taught by two Tibetan Buddhist Lamas. Having nothing else to do and not expecting much, I went. I was quite surprised when the teachings by Ven. Lama Yeshe and Ven. Zopa Rinpoche started answering the questions that had been with me since childhood. Reincarnation and karma explain how we got here. The fact that attachment, anger and ignorance are the source of all our problems explains why people do not get along and why we are dissatisfied. The importance of having a pure motivation shows that there is an alternative to hypocrisy. The fact that it is possible for us to abandon completely our faults and develop our talents and good qualities limitlessly gives purpose to life and shows how we can become a person who is really able to be of service to others.

The more I checked what the Buddha said, the more I found that it corresponded to my life experiences. We were taught practical techniques for dealing with anger and attachment, jealousy and pride, and when I tried them, I found that they helped my daily life go better. Buddhism respects our intelligence and does not demand blind faith - we are encouraged to reflect and examine. Also, it emphasizes changing our attitudes, not just giving a religious appearance on the outside. All this appealed to me.

There was a nun leading the meditations at this course, and it impressed me that she was happy, friendly, and natural, not stiff and "holy" like many Christian nuns I had met as a child. But still I thought that being a nun was strange - I liked my husband far too much to even consider it!

Being very moved by Buddha's teachings, I encouraged my husband to go to a meditation course in Indiana while I did a meditation retreat. He agreed, and touched by the teachings, he also took refuge. For me, this short retreat was a time to look inside myself, to check life's meaning, and to view life from a broader perspective. I thought deeply about our human potential, especially the fact that we can become Buddhas. I considered also the fact that death is certain, the time of death is uncertain, and that at death, our possessions, friends, relatives and body - everything that ordinary people spend their entire life living for - do not and cannot come with us. Knowing that the Dharma is something extremely important, and not wanting to miss the opportunity to learn it, after the retreat I suggested to my husband that we go to Nepal where Lama Yeshe and Zopa Rinpoche have a monastery. My husband did not want to go, but I was insistent, and in the end he agreed.

In October, 1975, we went to Kopan Monastery, near Kathmandu, Nepal, and attended another meditation course. Now I was taking a good look at my life, from the perspective of the Dharma. At deathtime, what do I want to have to show for my life? It was clear that my mind was overwhelmed by attachment, anger and ignorance. Everything I did was grossly or subtly under the influence of a selfish attitude. Due to the karmic imprints being collected on my mind stream through such actions and thoughts, it was clear that a good rebirth was extremely unlikely. And if I really wanted to help others, it was impossible to do so if I were selfish, ignorant and unskilful.

I wanted to change; the question was: "How?" Although many people can live a lay life and practice the Dharma, I saw that for me it would be impossible, simply because my afflictive emotions were too strong and my lack of self-discipline too great. Ordination seemed to be the best thing for my type of personality. I spoke with Lama Yeshe about this, and he told me to wait a while. As circumstances worked out, my husband had to go back to the U.S. in January, 1977, and I decided to go too to see my parents who had been upset by my letter saying that I wanted to become a nun.

My family did not understand why I wanted to take ordination: they knew little about Buddhism and were not very spiritually-inclined themselves. They did not comprehend how I could leave a promising career, marriage, friends, family, financial security and so forth in order to be a nun. It was a difficult time for everyone. I listened and considered all of their objections. But when I reflected upon their objections in terms of the Dharma, my decision to become a nun only became firmer. It became more and more clear to me that happiness does not come from having material possessions, good reputation, loved ones, physical beauty. Having these while young does not guarantee a happy old age, a peaceful death, and certainly not a good rebirth. If my mind remained continually attached to these things, how could I develop my potential and help others? It saddened me that my parents could not accept my decision, but I remained firm, with the thought to be of benefit to more people for a longer period of time. Ordination does not mean rejecting one's family. Rather, I wanted to enlarge my family and develop impartial love and compassion for all beings. With the passage of time, my parents have come to accept my being Buddhist and being a nun, for they see that not only am I happier, but also that what I am doing is beneficial to others.

My husband had ambivalent feelings: as he was a Buddhist, the wisdom side of him supported my decision, while the attachment side bemoaned it. It was difficult for him, but he took it as an opportunity to practice the Dharma. Now he is a successful lawyer in Los Angeles, and a devoted member of the Buddhist center there. Remarried, he has two children, and all of us get along well together.

Zopa Rinpoche then gave permission for me to be ordained. I returned to India, and in the spring of 1977, with much gratitude and respect for the Triple Gem and my Gurus, took ordination from Kyabje Ling Rinpoche, the senior tutor of His Holiness the Dalai Lama.

People ask if I have ever regretted this. No, not at all. I earnestly pray to the Triple Gem to keep my ordination purely and to be able to be ordained in future lives as well. Having vows is not restricting. Rather, it is liberating, for we become more determined not to do actions that, deep in our hearts, we do not want to do anyway. Although life is not always smooth - not because the

Dharma is difficult, but because the afflictive emotions are sneaky and tenacious - with effort, there is progress and happiness.

The early years of ordination were spent studying and meditating in Nepal and India. As Lama Yeshe and Zopa Rinpoche have a network of international Buddhist centers, they began sending the Western Sangha to help and to continue our studies and practice there. Thus, I have spent nearly two years at the center in Italy and three years at the monastery in France. When people asked the English-speaking Sangha to teach, our Gurus encouraged us to do so. Although I have no experience of the Dharma and extremely little knowledge, when asked to, I try to repeat what my teachers so kindly imparted. This has led me to various countries in Europe, Hong Kong, India and now Singapore. However, the essence of the Dharma remains the same everywhere, and for this reason, I try as much as possible to develop the compassion which cherishes others more than oneself and the wisdom which knows the ultimate nature of existence.

Lyn Riddett was born in 1941 in Sydney, Australia. She received her Ph.D from James Cook University in Townsville and is now Lecturer in Australian Studies at Northern Territories University in Darwin.

Dhamma - The Challenge and the Invitation

Lyn Riddett

In June 1986 I filled in an Australian government census form and in the section for ethnicity I wrote Irish-Australian, in the section for religion I wrote Buddhist. It was the first time I had written myself into those categories, and I was in fact making quite a strong statement, for my own benefit, about how I identified myself.

I am an Irish-Australian Buddhist, female and 47 years old. I have been Irish-Australian all my life. How long have I been a Buddhist? I honestly do not know, but I can date some of the times I heard about the Buddha and Buddhism.

The very first time was probably in 1949 when I was in Grade III at a Catholic primary school in Sydney. Our history text book had sections in it which dealt with non-western societies and cultures and there were stories for us to read about Buddha and Confucius. I remember having difficulty in sorting out who was who and where they came from. At the same time, however, as I recall, there was a tone of respect in my teacher's voice which convinced me that, although these men were not divine as Jesus Christ was, they were very good men. We were led to be sympathetic towards their followers because they had not had the opportunity of hearing the word of God. The nun taught us that through no fault of their own, these people were not baptised Christians and so could not go to heaven, but because of their goodness they would not be punished. Where would they go after death? I do not remember, except having some hazy idea of a second-class heaven reserved for non-Christians.

Despite the obvious compassion of the good women who taught us these things, I felt that what she was telling us was unjust. And later I was upset to find that during the Holy Week liturgy we were expected to pray for heathens and pagans as if they had done something wrong. These were early impressions and the sense of the Buddha and his teachings faded. They were not important in my life.

Many years later, during the 1960's, I was once again made aware of Buddhism by some of the events in the Vietnam War. Two particular images come to mind. The first is the television footage of Buddhist monks self-immolating in the streets of Saigon; the second is a conversation at a dinner party at my home in 1965. During that discussion one of my guests made the point that war would soon be over and that the Americans would win because most Vietnamese were Buddhists and Buddhists, he insisted, were expressly forbidden to kill. How could they, he argued, be expected to train as efficient soldiers if they were reluctant to take up arms?

The impact of the first image was shocking and I could not understand the calm and peace of the men who sat crosslegged on the roadway, poured petrol over themselves and then set themselves on fire. But I had some means of coming to terms with the second image - these soldiers who might fire in the air rather than at someone - means provided by my own family and our 'Irishness'.

We believed that part of Ireland was wrongly occupied by the British and I had been brought up to believe strongly in a free and united Ireland. At the same time something not quite explicitly stated by anyone in my family led me to believe that killing was very wrong. War was wrong. So what could an occupied nation do? At the time of the Vietnam War I was fascinated that another society faced this dilemma and that religious, or spiritual principles were an important factor in the situation. Somehow it seemed fitting that a nation should have to deal with spiritual matters while undertaking military and political action to resolve matters of sovereignty. These perceptions led me to realise, as well, that we had no business being in Vietnam because we had no adequate means of understanding the issues which had caught the Vietnamese up in the war.

At the same time as this was happening I was slowly and finally coming to terms with the fact that I was not a Catholic. I believed I was still a Christian, however, and in a general sense followed the teachings I had been given during childhood and adolescence. But the forms were meaningless for me, that is, they had no practical value in my life. Gradually I ceased to belong. My feeling at the time was that, unlike many of my friends who had lived through deep personal crises in 'leaving the Church', I had not left the Church. In some way, not clear to me, the Church had left me. If, at the time, I was on a path towards Buddhism, I did not know it and definitely had no feeling of having to replace one set of religious values with another. Neither did I know, because characteristically I continued to refuse to face squarely the dilemmas I was creating in my own life, that I was on a path which was to lead to twenty years of non-peace personally. It was at the end of those twenty years that I came finally to Buddhism, but the path was very wobbly and I did not understand for more than fifteen years what I needed to do to help myself. I know I needed to do something and tried many things: some taught me lessons I failed to heed; others led me deeper into distress and restlessness.

Two main events stand out: I separated from my husband and after an extremely difficult two years we were divorced; and in 1970, I went to live at Daguragu with a group of Aboriginal people who were fighting for the right to hold title to their traditional country. These people were strong, aggressive without being belligerent, firm in their purpose, compassionate towards the 'foreign occupiers' of their land, deeply pained and sometimes bitter as a result of their experience of colonialism, and deeply spiritual. The strongest and clearest of them were also very intuitive and wise. I believed some of them to be gifted with prescience, but I am inclined now to see them as being particularly aware and insightful people.

At this time, and for the whole of the 1970s, I suppose I was learning to unlearn cultural values that tied me into an Anglo-Celtic world view and which allowed me to continue to look outside myself for answers and solutions. I needed to unlearn this peculiarly western way of seeing and doing things before I could begin to learn how to sort myself out. The process of unlearning during the four years I was in contact with the people at Daguragu (I lived there for 13 months on and off during that time) was very painful. It became no less easy once I began to reinvolve myself in my own community. I made matters harder for myself because I kept avoiding what seems now to be the obvious, that is to look in, to become aware and to accept responsibility.

Like a lot of my friends, I arrived at the final stages of the path to Buddhism through a physical process. In trying to heal my body, by attempting to redress years of intemperate living, I came to see that something more than mere physical well-being was at stake. So the years of giving up began: nicotine, sugar, salt, alcohol excess (not completely), and the years of yoga and yogic meditation, and the years of 'gestalt' therapy. Not all of them were a waste, but I can see now that an emphasis on free expression of feelings, positive and negative, was for me quite counter-productive. My needs? To become quiet, to learn slowing down, to see more clearly, to accept and, most importantly, to let go. Other Buddhists will probably smile at that list and recognise delusion, hatred and greed in there. So, I suppose I also needed to learn that I am human and like other humans, subject to those three problems.

During these years, I gathered some more images about Buddhism, or more correctly, about Buddhists. Once again, two stood out.

In the late 1970s there was a television series about the main world religions, and naturally one part of that series was about Buddhism. The series' narrator visited Sri Lanka, and while he was there he spoke to members of the Sangha and to lay people. A woman told him that although it was perhaps sad that he was not born a Buddhist in this life, he was such a good person that more than likely he would be born Buddhist in his next incarnation. I was reminded of my teacher in Grade III, and so the connecting threads were revealed. Having been brought to the surface, this thread in my life began to be more important over the next six or seven years.

The second image was to be more directly significant. At the end of the segment on Buddhism, a monk is shown in walking meditation. Each time I see this part of the film, I am moved by the same feeling of awe and respect for the discipline and centredness implicit in the monk's action, and by the tranquility obvious in his face. And these were the qualities I found attractive in devout Buddhists I met, to the extent that I began to see that perhaps something in the Buddhist teaching might help me find the same tranquility. The qualities - quiet, dignity, physical ease, tranquility and compassion - are the ones I see still in Buddhists I know, and which I find worthwhile.

In 1983 I began slowly to practise the Buddha's teaching and in 1986 began reciting the three Refuges and the five Precepts. What do I find now that I am more or less on the Buddhist path? Relief. It has been a great relief to discover that I do not have to look beyond myself for answers to my problems, to find that I am responsible for my life and that no external agent needs to be placated or appealed to. I find the teachings very practical in helping me sort out priorities, in helping me solve my conflict, and useful in the most unexpectedly mundane ways in everyday life. Meditation does not come easily, but the benefits are so obvious I am not sure why I resist meditating each day - and I do resist, but I observe my resistance and come to a clearer understanding of myself as a result. Loving kindness meditation is a very *practical* way to organise my life which is busy and often stressful because of my workplace. The Buddhist Society in my community is comprised of people from many nationalities, and it offers me an opportunity to meet these people on common ground, and learn from them.

My life has not been changed radically by my acceptance of the Buddha's teachings. I was a person who needed to be brought into touch with a quiet, slow and peaceful revolution; radical change would have been disruptive and counter-productive in my case. Buddhism, by being available, by not proseletysing, by teaching insight and compassion and loving kindness and acceptance, and by presenting a centuries-old, tested tradition of interlocking philosophy and psychology, presented me with a challenge and an invitation. In the end I felt I had to accept both.

Karma Lekshe Tsomo was born in the United States in 1944. She received a B.A. in Oriental Languages from the University of California, Berkeley, and an M.A. in Asian Studies from the University of Hawaii as an East West Center Scholar. She subsequently studied for five years at the Library of Tibetan Works and Archives in Dharamsala, India. She received her novice ordination in France in 1977 and her higher ordination in Korea in 1982. Currently she is engaged in the study of Prajnaparamita at the Institute of Buddhist Dialectics in Dharamsala. She is co-director of the Tibetan Nuns' Project and of Sakyadhita, the International Association of Buddhist Women.

Choosing a Path

Karma Lekshe Tsomo

As a young child growing up, I was deeply attracted to things spiritual, particularly the ideal of practicing loving kindness. My mother tried her best to instill in me the qualities of morality and compassion as expressed in her Christian faith, and for this I am immensely grateful. Although I am still far from embodying these qualities, it was truly a blessing to be guided towards these true human values from a young age.

At thirteen, I began a phase of disillusionment on many levels. My home environment was ablaze and I was being separated from my dearest friend, my only brother; there was nothing I could rely on. There did not seem to be many people in the affluent church I was attending who lived up to Christ's injunction to give up everything and follow the spiritual path. Religion had apparently been relegated to a fairly routine Sunday morning affair, and did not provide what I was looking for.

Singing in the choir at church, I longed for experience beyond the worldly, yet kept running up against the prosaic nature of daily existence and my own failings. Being quite naughty by nature, I was caught in a bind between virtuous ideals and the reality of human imperfection. I had no clue as to how to reconcile the two.

Reeling between bewilderment and despair, heightened by grief over the death of my dog, I happened across a book on Zen Buddhism. I have never been able to determine exactly how it came into my hands, but I remember clearly the burnt, bronze-coloured cover of the book, which was called *The Way of Zen* by Alan Watts. My curiosity in the subject had already been kindled since my Prussian family name was Zenn. Intrigued, I found as I read that every line rang a chord of truth and familiarity. From then on, I began a search to understand more about Buddhism.

During my high school years I was busy cheerleading, surfing and raising rabbits, but I was also doing a lot of inner searching and had trouble finding answers to some very persistent questions. What happened to a person after death? Was the after-death state eternal? And were heaven and hell the only two possible alternatives? Why were people so unkind to each other? Why were the people around me so miserable and alcoholic when they possessed such wealth and every imaginable worldly advantage? Was there no other way to go through life than to contend tooth and claw for material gain? What was the point of this life anyway?

My brother and I had struggled intensely with such dilemmas as human evolution and the nature of perception. We could not really accept that we came from monkeys, but then how did we get here and why? We would debate endlessly about whether what he saw and labeled red or green was the same thing that I saw and labeled red or green (only to discover years later that he was colour blind!)

As I searched the libraries and second-hand bookshops for insights and guidance in meditation, I had a difficult time finding a clear path. It was 1959, and very little Buddhist literature was available. About all I could come up with were the fantasy escapades of Lobsang Rampa and some Theosophical tracts. When I finally came across some sutras translated from Pali, they instructed me to go live in solitude in the forest like an elephant and to be virtuous, both of which were way beyond my capacities at the time.

Seeking a spiritual direction in America amidst the reverence for material abundance of the 1950's was a lonely process. Acquisitiveness seemed so futile somehow, since acquisition brought no satisfaction and only multiplied people's problems. The spiritual life seemed much more attractive, but was I the only person who felt that way? Another decade would pass before Buddhist sensibilities began to evoke consideration among a larger circle of people in America. Nonetheless, from the very beginning, the Buddhist perception of human experience rang a true chord that resonated with my own inclinations.

One of the first concepts that impressed me as true was that of infinite time and space. Modern physicists are now close to accepting the Buddha's explanation of cosmic immensity, but at that time, it was a revolutionary notion, even heretical. To my mind, however, this expanded view of time and space sounded quite sensible, and the theory of rebirth fell logically into place with it.

The law of cause and effect struck me as a reasonable explanation for evolution. The theory of a creator god seemed illogical, because a god would itself require a cause, a creator. Surely, I felt, beings did not evolve only due to external conditions, but in response to their own process of inner development as well.

Another Buddhist teaching that appealed to me was that of renunciation. In the years since then, I have developed a genuine appreciation for certain material conveniences, but when first exposed to Buddhism, I was reacting against the gross and blatant adulation of possessions and the questionable methods people sometimes used to gain them. The Buddha's praise of the unattached life was encouraging to me.

The search for spiritual direction continued until I seemed to have exhausted all the possibilities the United States had to offer. Finally, feeling thoroughly alienated and disgusted by social corruption, American politics, crass materialism and overcrowded beaches, I determined to go to Japan to surf with some friends. So it was that in 1964, at the age of nineteen, I travelled to Japan with my surfboard to seek unexplored beaches and, I hoped, a fresh view of life.

The beaches were lovely and still unspoiled in those days, but a greater challenge presented itself in tracing the thread of Buddhist perception in the lives of ordinary people in Japanese society. Through reading and observing, I became absorbed in Zen culture and meditation. Still, it was difficult for me to integrate the practice into real life: the meditation hall and the subway crowds seemed in mutual contradiction. Without the guidance of a personal master, there was a danger of becoming lost in my own inner world. In the meantime, I took the Buddha's teachings as my guide.

One aspect of renunciation in particular struck me as relevant: the renunciation of partnership and family life. Normally, even in mid-20th century American society, the lot of a woman was to become a wife and mother. As unappealing as the prospect was in view of the immediate chaos of the families around me, it seemed useless to struggle against societal expectations. Luckily my parents did not push me into marriage, yet such a fate seemed almost unavoidable. The Buddha, however, was a monk. His example filled me with inspiration and hope.

Yet another feature of the Buddhist path that attracted me was its peacefulness. The Buddha did not advocate unreasoned pacifism to the extent of allowing oneself to become victimized, but he frequently offered advice as to how anger could be diffused and violence averted. Grieved by the ravages and suffering of recent wars, I felt gratitude and respect for a creed which offers solutions for establishing world peace. The Buddha taught meditation for creating inner serenity which then contributes to communal harmony. Even if it was not an overnight remedy to interpersonal and international conflicts, it seemed the most constructive and viable method I had yet encountered.

In short, I would say that my reasons for choosing the Buddhist path were equally personal, spiritual and philosophical. On the personal level, the Buddhist teachings showed me a way to simplify my life and gain inner happiness. They helped me to create more amicable and meaningful human relationships. On the spiritual level, the teachings guided me in very practical ways on the path of purification which ultimately leads to the state of enlightenment. They provided effective techniques to transform negative states of mind and to generate positive attitudes instead. Every stage of the way offers new insights and helps remedy beings' present confusion and discontent. On the philosophical level, the teachings set forth guidelines which helped me to discover for myself the answers to questions concerning birth and death, as well as the meaning of existence, the workings of the human mind, the riddles of human emotions and the process by which beings ultimately achieve realisation and liberation.

Thus I found that the Buddhist path satisfied my personal search, spiritual longings, and philosophical quandaries, all in one. At that point I took refuge from the heart and put my spiritual and personal development in the hands of the Buddha, Dharma and Sangha.

Wong Phui Weng was born in Malaysia in 1936. He was educated at the Victoria Institution in Kuala Lumpur, and later at the University of Malaya where he received a Ph.D in Botany. Mr. Wong has been active in promoting the study of Buddhism in Bahasa Malaysia, Malaysia's national language.

A Gift without Price

Wong Phui Weng

Although I was born into a nominally Buddhist family, I did not come into contact with the Dhamma until nine years ago. Since that time the teachings of the Buddha have changed my life, and I have many times felt regret that I did not come across them earlier.

My parents had minimal influence on me as far as religion was concerned, as my mother died when I was three years old and my father when I was seven. Under circumstances of great difficulty, I was brought up by my grandmother, who operated a canteen in a small Chinese school in Kuala Lumpur. My grandmother and my nursemaid continually stressed the importance of education, and it was drummed into me that my main goal in life was to do well in my studies. On certain days of the year, we worshipped Kuan Yin, the Bodhisattva of Compassion, and I picked up from my grandmother a vague idea about kamma, that good begets good and evil begets evil. This was virtually the only Buddhist influence in my upbringing.

Despite this, I remember having an interest in religion and I read any books I could get hold of. But as Buddhist literature was virtually non-existent and Christian literature plentiful, I read much of Christianity. The outcome of this was that I joined the Methodist Church and was baptised when I was seventeen. In the church there were opportunities to study and learn and I found the support

129

of like-minded people very helpful. I took my new religion seriously. However, in time, as I read the Bible more carefully, I found that I could not accept all of its teachings and my faith started to wane. I continued to read the Bible from time to time, drawing strength from the parts which I could accept and using the ethical teachings that appealed to me as a rough guide to my life.

I continued like this, giving only occasional thought to religion until my mid-thirties, when material success and the maturity of middle-age gave me time once again to think about religion. I found that although I now had economic security, I still did not understand the meaning of life and I was not as happy as I thought I should be. So once again I turned to Christianity, not, I now realise, because I thought it was better than other religions, but because there was plenty of literature on the subject and plenty of people who were more than willing to explain its doctrine to me and answer my questions. This time I studied under the guidance of a Catholic nun whose patience, kindness and deep faith impressed me deeply. I passed catechism, was baptised and again began attending church. But I still had nagging doubts about some of the central doctrines of Christianity. I think I continued to call myself a Catholic more out of a need to belong than out of deep conviction. I thought that if I continued to study and pray, my faith would grow. I read Christian literature listlessly, and yoga philosophy and the *Bhagavad Gita* with some interest, but none of it appeared to me to be the complete truth.

Then in 1979 the turning point of all this searching and inquiry finally came - I found a teaching that I could accept. A friend of mine had lost his job and I managed to help him find a new one. He said he wanted to give me something as an expression of his gratitude but I told him it was not necessary. After all, I had money enough to buy practically anything I needed. His response was to give me a small booklet called "Sayings of the Buddha". The booklet, published by the Buddhist Missionary Society, cost only ten cents and contained extracts from the *Dhammapada* and other Buddhist scriptures. My friend told me it was a gift without price and that I would find it interesting even though I was a Catholic. But so influenced was I by the idea that reading the literature of other religions was wrong, that I put this little booklet aside. Three months later when I finally decided to browse through it, I immediately felt that the Buddha must be the greatest and the fairest of men and that I must find out more about his wonderful teachings. The second line in my friend's booklet impressed me most deeply of all. It said: "There is truth in every religion. Accept it when you find it." I was delighted by the broad-mindedness of this statement and that someone could be confident enough about their own religion to say such a thing. I became a Buddhist and have remained one, growing more enthusiastic about the Dhamma the more I read it. And all because of a little ten-cent booklet. My friend was right. It was a gift without price.

Bhikkhu Nyanasobhano was born in the United States in 1948. He was educated at Dartmouth College. He was ordained as a Buddhist monk in 1987, and now resides at the Vietnamese Buddhist Temple in Washington, D.C.

A Buddhist and Glad

Bhikkhu Nyanasobhano

For years now, acquaintances have looked surprised and quizzical on learning that I am a Buddhist. It is not simply that Buddhists are relatively rare in America (so are believers in a hundred other faiths), but Buddhism is, in the popular mind, linked with the exotic East, with the strange and outlandish. It is not too surprising that Asian immigrants should continue to follow the religion, but that a native-born *American* should adopt it and unapologetically profess it baffles quite a few people. I do not say I have an "interest" in Buddhism (which would be merely colourful) but instead say, if asked about it, that I *am* a Buddhist. This often excites curiosity, not so much about the religion as about the process by which I came into it - as if I must be a very odd person to have gone so far afield in search of truth. It does not seem so remarkable to me, though I admit that the search and its results have been profoundly meaningful for me. I look back, and the events unroll in my mind like old maps that might lead to the source for this condition of faith. Some trends and tendencies show up, but *all* the causes for a condition cannot be known. The universe is not yet exhausted of mystery.

I grew up in a suburban environment in Louisville, Kentucky, U.S.A., with a wide variety of boyish enthusiasms. Religion was not one of them. Although I was brought up in the Presbyterian Church, I never developed any attachment to it or its doctrines. I knew that religion was supposed to be something important, but I seldom gave it much thought, as it did not seem at all relevant to my life. I had not developed the faculty of thinking critically and was merely drifting along on instinct.

This changed when I reached age fifteen or sixteen and was introduced to serious literature. I had always loved reading, and when I encountered at school the work of writers who were really concerned about the big questions of human existence, I began to examine those same questions myself with awakening interest. Art and philosophy and literature seemed to lead away into uncharted territories that promised beautiful revelations. Any youth wants to know about the physical world, but for the first time I realized there was an intellectual, or perhaps spiritual, dimension that could also be known. Religion rose to the surface of my consciousness as a result of these new ruminations on life, death, and fate, but mostly in an unfavourable light. I now began to criticize on logical - or what I thought were logical - grounds the religious explanations that before had simply bored me, and quite soon I rejected them altogether. Whether my reasoning was accurate or not, it was effectual, and from that point on regarded myself as a free-thinker browsing through the fields of knowledge.

During my high school years, I read a lot of wonderful literature, plus science fiction novels and oddities of all descriptions, and I developed intermittent enthusiasms for subjects like Yoga, hypnotism, psychic phenomena, and so on. I also read a little bit about various Eastern religions, mostly searching for tales of miracles and exalted states of mind, and I remember a passing acquaintance with Buddhism, though I probably had only the dimmest understanding of its teaching. I did not feel any "religious" impulse at all, only a passionate appetite for experience of an adventurous and mind-expanding nature.

I went off to college with the goal of becoming a writer and setting the literary world on its ear. During my four years there in the late 1960's I was immersed in the "youth culture" but actually felt little sympathy for the hippies and the artistic and cultural ferment they represented. I wished to break limits but I was not about to abandon the life of the intellect. As I had not come across any single philosophy to arrest my faith, I continued for a few years after college to regard myself as a romantic poet and philosopher following my own path. I had never taken a college course in religion, and continued largely indifferent to religions as organized systems of belief. I enjoyed poetic bits of wisdom but preferred to collect them from many sources - a very prevalent habit, I now realize.

Out on my own, I was obliged to support myself with a series of low-paying jobs while I worked on my writing. I also became an actor and worked frequently on the stage for a number of years. This was occasionally exciting but more often tedious and full of anxiety. It was an up-and-down kind of life, and I faintly suspected there was another kind, a better kind, which was beyond the bounds of what I had hitherto known. So that at the same time as I was trying to be a "Renaissance man" with myriad accomplishments, I was quietly looking for a deeper and more solid level of reality. I took to reading books on Yoga and meditation in hopes of discovering an effective technique for freeing my mind from its old restraints and exploring the greater world. The books promised a lot, and told marvellous stories of adepts who attained mystical insight of one kind or another. I had no way of judging the truth of such assertions, but I thought that some of them *might* be true - since I had what I now think was a genuine intuition of the higher life of wisdom - so I began to meditate according to my own hazy, haphazard inclinations and the often incomprehensible instructions in the books.

I found most references to meditation in books on Buddhism, of which there were a few in the Louisville public library. I would study these, then sit on the floor of my apartment and imagine myself accomplishing prodigies of concentration. Nothing spectacular happened. Usually I felt a little calmer afterwards, at least enough to wish to continue this line of practice. I was chiefly interested in techniques and magnificent results, so that it was only gradually that the philosophies behind the techniques made their way into my consciousness. But at length, I began to realize that Buddhism was a comprehensive philosophy that spoke of many of the inarticulate urges and notions I had all my life. My interest focused on Zen Buddhism for a time, because almost all the books I saw were about that and because I was attracted to the artistic, aesthetic elements in Zen, as well as its amusing paradoxes. But eventually I grew restless with Zen's vagueness and lack of specificity. I wanted some concrete instructions on how to meditate, so, in my library wanderings I one day picked up a book with a section on Theravada Buddhist meditation and theory. My interest immediately quickened when I saw that here was a clear, progressive programme of meditation, a down-to-earth, rational system that claimed to lead gradually, step by step, to that most mysterious and alluring state - "enlightenment". Further investigation of Theravada Buddhism revealed it to be a grand system of thought that not only explained the *how* of meditation but the *why* as well, and at last I began to understand that the *why* was important - was, in fact, indispensable to any spiritual progress.

In slowly digesting the ethics and philosophy of the Dhamma, the original teachings of the Buddha, I lost something of my extravagant appetite for wondrous mental experiences. Before I could ascend to the heights, I had to take stock of where I actually was, of the situation of myself as an individual and a mortal being among billions of others. The majestic Four Noble Truths of Buddhism, which before I had skipped over, struck me with increasing force. The *why* of religious practice must be this pervasive and inescapable suffering - all else was whim and ignorance. The Buddha's summary was brilliant: there is this omnipresent unsatisfactoriness of disease; it has a cause and the cause is craving; by removing the cause one can bring all suffering to an end; and there is a path of living that can accomplish this goal. As I entertained these teachings intellectually, turning them over and over in my mind, I could not help noticing in the world around me and in my own sorrows and frustrations much of what the Buddha was talking about. My youthful romanticism was wearing thin, wearing almost transparent, one might say, and through it I could see the ceaseless rising and falling of enthusiasms, projects, interests, hopes, and so on. A suspicion of the futility even of the artistic life stole over me. Life rolled on from one day to the next, bringing relative joy or sorrow, but these experiences *did not last*. They were impermanent, and in their impermanence, they did not seem to offer any kind of conclusion other than dull death. Before my eyes, in the parade of my own and others' lives, was the suffering and impermanence declared by the Buddha. It seemed I might have to take up his discipline in earnest if I wanted to avoid my probable fate.

I did not consider myself a Buddhist - the thought scarcely crossed my mind - but I continued to ponder the Dhamma and certainly devoted more energy to meditation. The refreshing clarity and at least initial simplicity of *vipassana* meditation caused me to keep at it and to lengthen my periods of sitting meditation. Did I get results? Certainly I saw no lights, heard no celestial sounds, felt no swooning intimations of ecstasy. But I did feel a growing sense of *rightness*, as if these humble, unglamorous investigations of mind and body, so far from the cerebral explosions I had craved, were lifting me inch by inch out of a deep ignorance.

In time, I grew tired of meditating out of a book, as it were, and wanted to go somewhere and meet somebody who could give me guidance in the practice. My studies till then had been almost completely solitary. One or two of my friends had a slight interest in meditation, but I knew no one who wanted to undertake it systematically, and certainly no one who had any deep knowledge of the business. So I wondered about going to one of the meditation retreats I had heard about in other cities. Learning that there was a Theravada Buddhist temple in Washington, D.C., I wrote to the people there, and after getting favourable responses to my inquiries I decided to visit Washington to sample real Buddhism. My summer employment as an actor had ended and there was no reason I could not undertake this small adventure.

So I went to Washington to visit and ended up staying for years. I was pleased with the Buddhism I found, and soon made the acquaintance of many monks and lay people at various temples in the area. I did get the meditation instruction I desired, but more than that, I got a grounding in the broad base of the Dhamma and saw how one part fits into another and leads logically into the practice of morality, concentration, and wisdom, with the ultimate aim being *nibbana*, deliverance from all sorrow. I did not immediately realize it, but I had crossed a bridge and could never go back to my old world-view. I felt supported, not only by fellow meditators, but also by the Dhamma itself, by the sheer momentum of moving even slowly on the path.

One time, not long after my arrival in Washington, I found myself awkwardly explaining to someone, "I'm a Buddhist - more or less." Afterwards I wondered, why this qualifier: "more or less"? Was I a Buddhist or wasn't I? Was I still equivocating, dabbling? I thought about it a while, and quite soon - it seemed the most natural thing in the world - I felt a surge of conviction and I realized there was no question about it: I was a Buddhist. I had made no great vows, suffered no ordeals of conscience, undergone no "conversion", but it had happened - I was a Buddhist.

Years have passed, and my appreciation of the Dhamma has deepened. Perhaps I see more clearly now what attracted me and continues to attract me to this practice and this way of life. In Buddhism, I found not only a prescription for healthy living, not only a gateway into meditational experience, but a thorough and rational explanation of how and why things work the way they do. To me and perhaps to most children of the atomic age, the unreflective abandon of unsupported faith was repellent. I wanted explanations that my own reason could follow. I wanted a straightforward explanation of reality that pointed the way - if a way there was - to the summits of spiritual achievement. I distrusted all gurus and the cults of devotion they fostered. I would not invest my devotion anywhere until I saw for myself that a belief or an ideal was demonstrable and logical and more than romantic puffery. In Buddhism I met a majesty of thought that awed me, and a freedom of investigation that was balm to my restless mind. Not only was I free to inquire, to doubt, I was *encouraged* to. The Buddha said that a student should analyse and test his words as carefully as a goldsmith tests gold. I was invited to see for myself and *then* believe out of my own experience. The Buddhist analysis of the world, of the operations of cause and effect, of the rational foundations of morality, and of the possibility for diminishing delusion made sense to me, and the more I reflected, the more I saw those principles manifest in the world. Everywhere in the Buddha's doctrine, I sensed a powerful understanding that cut through the fumes of misperception to the actual nature of mental and physical events and the problems of existence. How many religious-minded people had simply given up trying to understand the tumultuous world and ducked under a cloud of belief? How many materialists had bitterly despaired of higher truth and spent their lives chasing their tails intellectually? But there was no need to go to either extreme. The world could both be known and transcended. In fact, by understanding the facts of everyday existence one could mount by degrees to the ineffable. Clearly, the Buddha had healed the split between intellect and spirit.

Buddhism is a dynamic religion. By this I mean that, on the one hand, it teaches the dynamism of the universe - its ceaseless turmoil, unrest, and impermanence - and on the other hand, it teaches a dynamic way of practice. We are not to sit around worrying about the state of our virtue as our days dwindle away; we are not just killing time until some fate - dreadful or glorious - overtakes us. On the contrary, we must *make* our fate. The doctrine of *kamma* beautifully explains the bewildering variety of worldly situations and in effect allows man a choice of futures. We have it within our power to direct our destiny through the kinds of deeds we perform, and, more than this, we can change ourselves for the better through the intelligent practice of the Noble Eightfold Path. Nothing, neither triumph nor tragedy, occurs spontaneously, out of nothing. The universe is ordered, and wisdom is the discovery of that order in experience, not just in theory. Buddhism provides a means to attain such wisdom and free ourselves gradually from self-defeating patterns of behaviour. There is suffering, the Buddha taught, and there is the ending of suffering.

Many Western Buddhists find in Buddhism a congenial spirit of scientific inquiry as well as a profound sense of wonder and beauty. There is room on this path for people of all abilities and levels of understanding, because Buddhism is, after all, a raft for ferrying one to the farther shore; it is a vehicle for learners - for those who wish to learn. If we were already free from weakness and ignorance there would be no need for this raft at all. So a Buddhist breathes a democratic atmosphere and feels the moral support of his fellow strivers, whatever their level of attainment. This has been clear to me all along, and is a source of encouragement. The Buddha overlooked no one in his compassion, and his teachings embrace all beings in all abodes.

This universal character of Buddhism particularly impressed me. Buddhism is truly a world religion. It is not confined to any particular continent, or race, or culture, because it deals with the fundamentals of existence which are the same everywhere. Quite a number of Americans and Europeans have become interested in Buddhism after living or travelling in Asia or by studying some Asian culture or art, but I was chiefly drawn by Buddhist teaching itself. Beyond a fondness for Chinese and Japanese painting and poetry, I had no special interest in Asia. I came into this religion because, although it is over 2,500 years old, it spoke directly and meaningfully to me as an individual, as it has to millions of others of incredibly diverse backgrounds.

I never *decided* to become a Buddhist, but only tried to follow what seemed to be the best course according to my understanding, and here I am, a Buddhist and glad of it. I revere the Dhamma because I have discovered it to be worthy of reverence. It seems to me that in this world oppressed by the heat and thirst of passions, this Dhamma is like water from a pure, cool spring - all may drink of it and all may be refreshed.